Leading The Way

Leading The Way

The Church or Culture?

Michael Youssef

Marshall Pickering

Marshall Pickering
3 Beggarwood Lane, Basingstoke, Hants RG23 7LP, UK

Edited by David J. Lee.

First published in 1986 by Marshall Morgan and Scott
Publications Ltd
Part of the Marshall Pickering Holdings Group
A subsidiary of the Zondervan Corporation

ISBN 0 551 01352 4   paperback
ISBN 0 551 01411 3   hardback

Phototypeset in Linotron Times, 11 on 12 pt
by Input Typesetting Ltd, London
Printed in Great Britain by
Camelot Press Ltd, Southampton, Hants.

Dedicated to
The Most Reverend Donald W B
Robinson, Archbishop of Sydney,
Australia, and Marie—two people
to whom I owe a debt of gratitude

CONTENTS

CONTENTS

I: CHURCH VS CULTURE: Taking a Stand

Next time you catch the flu, or wind up an old grandfather clock, or pick up a pair of field glasses, spare a thought for Galileo.

It was Galileo who invented the thermometer. He also developed the pendulum, and designed the first telescope to watch the stars. And he did one far more important thing, too—he overturned the old, outdated view of the universe and replaced it with the one we have today.

Before Galileo, nearly everyone believed that the earth stood at the centre of the universe; everything else—the sun, the moon, the stars—revolved around it. What could be more sensible or self-evident? After all, you could see the sun travelling in its great arc across the heavens and the moon sliding through the sky at night.

Standing on the ground, it didn't feel as if you were moving anywhere. And, anyway, didn't it stand to reason that, since God had put man on the earth, this was clearly the most important spot in space and so deserved to be in the middle?

Be that as it may, said Galileo, no, the earth is not in the middle. In fact, it revolves around the sun.

He was not the first person to come up with this, then extraordinary, idea. It had been propounded a century earlier by another scientist, Nicolas Copernicus, and is thus called the Copernican, as well as the heliocentric, system.

Naturally it was a great step forward, both for man's understanding of the world and for science generally. But that didn't make it popular, and so far as the church was concerned it was second only to heresy. Galileo was picking away at the foundations of a huge edifice of official dogma that the church was in no hurry to dismantle even though, as a matter of strict science, Galileo happened to be right in many respects. Consequently he met persistent opposition and was finally threatened with the inquisition if he did not recant.

It was not until the time of Isaac Newton a century later that the lost ground in astronomy began to be made up.

Why did it happen? The simple answer is probably: it's human nature.

The church has often rejected new ideas because they represent the unknown; they challenge long standing prejudices and threaten vested interests. If we are satisfied with things the way they are we will not take kindly to someone upsetting the status quo. We fear change coming and resent it long after it has arrived.

We have only to examine the pages of history to find the same story played out again and again.

Right back at the beginning of church history Christians were divided over circumcision. All of Christ's first disciples were Jews; for them Christianity was the fulfilment and completion of religious convictions they already held, that there was one God, who created the world and saved his people.

But of course when the Apostle Paul took the Gospel to the Gentiles the question immediately arose whether it was necessary to be a Jew before you could be a Christian—whether, to come down to practicalities, Gentile believers required circumcision.

Paul's own affirmation that salvation is by faith, not works, argued against the judaization of the Christian converts, but there were many who disagreed with him. It took the first church council at Jerusalem and the formal support of Peter and James to free gentile Christians from the yoke of Jewish custom. Even then the ruling was far from universally accepted, as Paul's letters show.

Much the same thing happened with all the great heresies of the first four centuries. Gnosticism, Montanism, and Docetism all came about because certain elements in the church could not reconcile their own ideas with the challenge of the gospel.

In a way, the disputes that followed were necessary if the church was going to hammer out its doctrines. Great thinkers rose to the occasion, among them Athanasius of Alexandria, bishop in what later became the Coptic Church in which I was brought up, who faced down the heresy of Arianism and gave us the Athanasian Creed.

But as time went on the church allowed the great scriptural teachings decided by its early councils to be buried beneath a structure that was worldly and materialistic. Given the privileges of power in the Empire it became like the Empire and treated its dissenters as traitors.

Men like Jon Hus, who claimed that the church had become corrupt and based their faith on the Scripture that church leaders had interpreted for their own convenience, were rewarded with death at the stake. Martin Luther escaped only because he enjoyed the protection of the German princes. The founding bishops of the Anglican Church—Latimer, Ridley and Cranmer—all burned in the religious divisions of Reformation England.

The Reformers wanted the one thing that the church was determined to resist: change.

And if you think that sort of blind obstinacy went out with the Reformation, think about this more recent example from the United States. Just prior to the Civil War the newly formed Southern Presbyterian Church held its first general assembly. The major issue for debate: Does the black man have a soul?

By modern standards it is an unexpected, almost unbelievable question—at the very least, one with a clear, biblical answer. For the southern Christians of that time, however, a good deal hung upon it. If they admitted that blacks had souls they were in effect saying there is no difference in spiritual terms between blacks and whites. Once that is granted, several embarrassing conclusions

follow. A black is a human being. He has as much right
to freedom as a white.

Therefore if you own a black man as a slave (and many
white southern Presbyterians did just that) you will either
have to pay him a fair wage or set him free—not a happy
prospect for a farmer whose profits relied on cheap
labour.

Even so, here was a rare opportunity for a large group
of Christians to get together and say, 'God is no respecter
of persons and we accept blacks as equal with whites.'
That they did not is a testimony to the power exercised
over them by their culture and economy, and a tragedy
that led to decades of misery.

What many of the Presbyterian whites did decide to do
was to fudge the issue, a very useful course of action
when morality fails to coincide with your personal interests. They opted for James Thornwell's doctrine of the
'spirituality of the church'. This meant, simply, that
because economics and politics happened outside the
walls of the church building, Christians were not bound
to think about them. Hence the abolition of slavery was
not their concern.

Christians today have the same kind of choice to make
as those Presbyterians of old did. All Christians of all
ages have had it. The issue is whether the influence
between church and culture bears upon the Christians or
the culture.

We can set the standards and take the lead, or we can
get pushed out of the way and compromised by the values
and opinions popular in the world around us. It is a clear
choice: on the one hand we regard the Bible as a source
of authority and take a firm stand on ethical issues; on
the other we are coloured by whatever views are current
and end up saying what everyone else is saying. (We may
add a garnish of allusion to Christian history or Scripture.) Since the second is not worthwhile, the options
really reduce themselves to speaking up or shutting up.

Sadly, in terms of influence between church and culture

in the twentieth century, the traffic has been almost all one way in the wrong direction.

Take capital punishment.

Until recently, criminal justice in most Western countries has run on the Old Testament principle of proportionate retribution—an eye for an eye and a tooth for a tooth. But the New Testament commandments of love, some have argued, negate this principle: no one has the right to deprive another human being of life, even as a punishment for taking life. As a result, some church bodies have taken an official stand against capital punishment, thus dividing the witness of the church and preventing it from speaking with a united voice.

Yet the traditional view, still put forward by some Christians, is that proportionate retribution is an eternal principle of life, clearly demonstrable from Scripture. Is it not the case, then, that the modern view has been influenced, even controlled, by the predominantly humanist culture?

The same point can be made about other issues with which I am dealing in this book. In each it is possible to trace a gradual abandonment of Biblical positions under the pressure of the prevailing culture. The church has become merely a lapdog of popular opinion.

The status of women is a typical example. For most of the twentieth century male predominance in the office and home has been under attack. The Second World War gave women the chance to prove themselves in industry while men were overseas.

This made a permanent change in their economic role. The working woman was here to stay.

It was then only a matter of time before this new independence sought expression in the church. Why, it was argued, should church leadership—an exclusively male preserve if ever there was one—be exempt from a change the rest of society was clearly accepting?

Finding no adequate response to this, churches began admitting women to leadership positions never open to them before. Of course, from there it was only a short step to ordination and an almost uncontrollable re-analysis of sex roles in Christianity. This has ridden rough-shod over those denominations that are unable to reconcile women's ordination with their interpretation of Scripture.

It has even resulted in a rewriting of the New Testament, where Jesus is portrayed as feminine as well as masculine.

A similar movement has occurred in the church's view of homosexuality. The church is 'responding' to our society's redefinitions of the condition as, first, an illness rather than a sin, and second, less an illness than the inevitable consequence of certain childhood experiences and environments.

Today gay liberation has established homosexuality as an alternative lifestyle no better or worse in a moral sense than the heterosexual. The Church, unwilling to step out of line with contemporary culture, has for the first time in twenty centuries begun to accept practising homosexuals into full membership.

Currently, the question is whether they should be ordained. If they are, there seems no substantial reason to object to making gay ordination a *necessity* to avoid discrimination—a ludicrous reversal of biblical teaching.

Time after time the same thing has happened: instead of leading and influencing the culture in which it exists, the church has lamely given in and followed, like a shepherd following his flock as it wanders aimlessly over the hills.

That is a tragedy for the church itself; but more than that, it is a betrayal of the responsibility it has for the surrounding culture.

When Jesus told His disciples to be the salt of the earth, He was referring to the practice of packing fish in rock salt for transportation. His disciples were to be for their times what the salt was for the fish—a preservative without which the cargo would go rotten.

Salt that had lost its saltiness was useless in preserving the fish and could only be tossed out for road-building.

This was an essential reminder for the disciples that their task was to hold off corruption in their culture and give it flavour—not to end up getting trodden on.

Being salt, of course, doesn't always mean influencing culture from the outside. There have been times when the opportunity has been there for the church to pick up a cause initiated *within* society. However, although it is quite receptive to *destructive* changes in the surrounding culture the church has often let *good* changes pass unnoticed.

When the government finally outlawed DDT, for instance, it was as a result of a secular environmentalist lobby and not the influence of the church. In spite of having good Scriptural grounds for criticizing exploitative use of pesticides, the church had said practically nothing about this. The same scenario has been repeated in regard to smoking and drunken driving.

Such failure follows very largely from an inability to distinguish between *change* and *progress*.

Change often finds expression as material goods. Change is replacing a black and white TV with a colour one; getting a video unit, a digital watch or a heart and lung transplant.

Since all of these things improve upon their predecessors, we are automatically predisposed to think that change is always for the better, that all change is *progress*. Since progress is clearly a good and desirable thing, it follows that change also must be good and desirable.

It then requires only a little specious moral argument (such as, 'It is unreasonable discrimination not to ordain homosexuals') to convince us that the benificence of change is universal. Hence the church is seduced into inactivity and fails to act as it should—as critic, leader, salt.

The fish are left to 'preserve' themselves!

But clearly not all change is progress. Galileo did us all a service with his thermometer and telescope, but is a lethal pesticide progress? And what about the thermonuclear bomb—is that progress?

It doesn't take much thought to show that changes of
any sort can be good *or* bad, depending upon how you
use them, and some changes are no good at all. Therefore
it is worth asking: Why is the church subscribing to the
change = *progress* myth? The true church mirrors Jesus
Christ, not the fads of a culture. It shapes society, it does
not allow society to shape it. It is a rock, not a sponge.

That doesn't mean Christians are opposed to change.
They should have accepted the early advances in
astronomy and physics with open arms, and it says a lot
about the flexibility of the Christian faith that it has ridden
the technological age in a way that more rigorous and
regional faiths like Islam have not. But it is God's change
we follow, not man's. We serve the same God who
showed Moses a cloud in the sky and led him onward.

Not that the Bible presents us with a blueprint of the
Christian social ideal to be followed blindly. Once again,
that distinguishes us from other religions: in every age
we listen to the myriad of voices and listen afresh to the
quiet speaking of the Holy Spirit as we seek to apply
the timeless, universal theological truths left to us in the
teaching of Jesus Christ.

And right at the centre of that process in every age will
be the Biblical insight that culture needs to be redeemed
by and through the Holy One who, though without sin,
was crucified like the worst offender. It is His example
that we follow, and it may sometimes be His fate that we
share. But that is the prophetic role of a church that
refuses to be carried along in the chaos of a culture, that
is willing to speak, to lead, to question and if necessary
to condemn.

History tells us of many such men and women.

One story concerns a monk called Telemachus who,
during the fifth century when the majority of people in
the Roman Empire had become professed Christians,
leaped into the arena to stop a gladiatorial combat. The
mob—presumably nominally Christian—were outraged
and stoned him to death for interfering with their
pleasure. Thereupon the Emperor ordered the spectacles

to be stopped and Telemachus enrolled among the martyrs. One man's sacrifice ended a cruel sport and changed the course of history.

That is the calling of the church and the pattern set for it by Christ Himself.

As Origen said in the second century, 'The blood of the martyrs is the seed of the church.' Yet in today's America, martyrdom is a rare calling, and the challenge facing us is at the same time less personal and more serious. Stated in the positive, our task is to speak out against evil with a clear biblical proclamation and to embody the good we stand for so that it may be emulated by others.

But it would be misleading to suggest this was optional, and so the challenge is far better stated in the negative: if Telemachus died to lead, we must lead—or die.

II: WOMEN: What do They Want?

The course of true love rarely runs smooth. So goes the old adage—but why should it be so? Professor Henry Higgins, in Shaw's *Pygmalion*, perhaps speaks for many men when he cries in exasperation: 'Women upset everything. When you let them into your life, you find that the woman is driving at one thing and you're driving at another.'

For centuries men have loved the fairer sex; they have admired and revered her—but they have never understood her. Even the father of psychoanalysis, Sigmund Freud—who must have stood a better chance than most of us—concluded on his deathbed:

> 'The question . . . which I have not been able to resolve . . . is, what does a woman want?' (quoted in Charles Rolo, *Psychology in American Life*, 1963.)

So, what *does* a woman want?

Modern feminism answers definitively: liberation. Women want to throw off the old male-dominated order and compete on an equal footing with men. That the movement should have gained the title Women's Lib demonstrates pretty clearly the strength of feeling behind it.

When Elizabeth Cady Stanton and Lucretia Mott promoted their bill of rights it was out of a deep conviction that women, as the full intellectual equals of men, deserved the same treatment and privileges. Today's feminists, given the independence of the pill, are if anything more radical. They have scored notable victories with the Equal Opportunities Act in Britain (1975) and the acquisition of power in local and state politics in the US.

But this throwing back into the melting pot of sexual roles has also resulted in confusion—particularly in the church. Many Christians are asking whether there is not some truth in this feminist assertion: Beneath a facade of religious respectability the churches conceal a blatant sexism that would not be tolerated in a secular institution.

The controversy focuses on two issues. One, which will be discussed in a separate chapter, is peculiar to the church and concerns the admission of women to the ministry. The second is universal: What is the correct definition of a woman's role in the family?

Both raise the same question for churches which before the twentieth century have had little reason to doubt their opinions on such matters. Put in its most basic form—is the teaching of the church on the role of women a faithful interpretation of scripture, or a sanctification of the male desire for dominance?

The question has to be followed through, and the best route is back to basics—the Greek, Roman and Judaic cultures that held sway when Christianity first appeared. Each civilization had developed its own particular attitudes regarding the role of women. The Christian outlook grew up between and in contradistinction to them all. It did not always have much in common with its predecessors.

Ask the average Greek in the Classical Age what he thought about the equality of the sexes and you'd have got the sort of blank stare people adopt nowadays watching a Japanese version of *Hamlet*. Women didn't register in any sense that would have made 'equality' a meaningful term. 'We have companions for our pleasure,' wrote Demosthenes, meaning courtesans,

'concubines for the daily needs of the body, and wives

so we may have legitimate children and a faithful
steward for our houses.' (quoted in Leonard Swidler,
Women in Judaism, Scarecrow Press, 1976.)

If Demosthenes was the original male chauvinist pig it
can be said in his defense that nearly every other Greek
chauvinist occupied the same sty, including Aristotle. But
not Plato. The *Republic* with its vision of women educated
and participating in government exudes a pleasant aroma
of liberalism:

'There is no occupation concerned with the manage-
ment of social affairs which belongs either to woman
or to man, as such. Natural gifts are to be found here
and there in both creatures alike' (tr. Francis
MacDonald Cornford, OUP, 1940).

In Roman society, attitudes and practices changed
considerably from the early days of the republic to the
height of the Roman Empire. Under the republic—a very
different one from Plato's—a father enjoyed rights over
his wife and children that were little short of totalitarian.

Women were generally regarded as weak and light-
minded. Married or not, a woman fell under the legal
authority and protection of a man—her husband or her
father. If the urge came upon him, he could kill her with
no questions asked.

Fortunately for the wives the Second Punic War put an
end to all that. New laws passed at the end of the war
prevented the passage of dowry rights from a bride's
father to her husband, with the result that women gained
greater control of property and more independence in
marriage. If the man still held the steering wheel, his wife
was now at least in the back seat and not in the trunk.

Ancient Rome was no less male-oriented than ancient
Greece, but had a different, more restrained attitude
toward sexuality. . . . They were considered mistresses
of the household and had inheritance rights which prod-

uced many wealthy widows. Marriages were indissol-
uble from the woman's side and difficult for men to
dissolve. This resulted in a more secure role for
women. . . .
Wealthy Roman women were educated to some
degree, a very different situation from that of most
Greek and Oriental women and while subject to their
husbands, whose rights over them and their daughters
extended even to execution, enjoyed the most favour-
able and respected position of all Mediterranean
women.
(James B. Hurley, *Man and Woman in Biblical
Perspective*, Zondervan, 1981.)

Israel was no less a patriarchal society than Greece or
Rome. But here a woman did have the advantage of a
moral as well as a judicial law which gave men explicit
responsibilities alongside their privileges. She could not
be divorced unless a husband could prove her promiscuity
(Deut.22). She was free—though admittedly by her
husband's consent—to make religious vows just like a
man (Num. 30).

Several women occupy places of prominence in the Old
Testament, but more often in positions of religious rather
than political authority. Deborah, Huldah, Moadiah and
the unnamed wife of Isaiah were all prophetesses. An
exception to the rule is the notorious Jezebel, the power
behind the throne of her weak husband Ahab.

Against the gradual reforms of Rome and the ancient
proscriptions of the Mosaic Law the attitude of Christ
appears almost revolutionary. As the bringer of the
Kingdom of God He treated women as they had never
been treated before—as the fundamental equals of men.
His recorded meetings with women in the Gospels show
no hint of the discrimination that would have been
customary for a male of His time.

In fact He went out of His way to break contemporary
taboos by speaking to women who by reason of
nationality or a disreputable profession no conscientious

Jew would have touched with a ten-foot pole. Women
were among His closest followers; they accompanied Him
on His travels, stood by Him in His death, and were first
to witness His resurrection. Their faith and devotion often
won them higher acclaim than many of the men who
sought His counsel.

What the church did with this extraordinary example
of its Founder varied a good deal. In the specific matter
of marital relationships Christians have tended towards
one of three different perspectives. Often one has been
emphasised at the expense of the other, with the result
that the church's view of marriage has become distorted.
Yet all three are necessary, and in my opinion there is
no reason why they should not be held in combination.
Each contains an essential ingredient of the truth.

The first perspective can be called **comparison**, the
recognition of differences in the nature and role of the
sexes. Into this category can be placed the following
observation from Martin Luther: 'Men have broad and
large chests, and small narrow hips, and more understanding than women, who have but small and narrow
chests, and broad hips, to the end they should remain at
home, sit still, keep house, and bear and bring up children.' (*Table Talk*, DCCXXV, 1569.).

How many women—or even men—would agree
nowadays that intelligence has some sort of relation to
the size of your chest is debatable. But that women bear
children and tend to be broader in the hip than men is
beyond dispute. Anyway, both statements are cast in the
form of a comparison.

Of course the blade cuts both ways: some feminists are
claiming now that women alone, as bearers and nurturers
of children, are capable of sustaining world peace. The
trouble with comparison is that once A and B have been
distinguished, one is inevitably ranked higher than the
other. In the ranking game, women have generally come
off worse because they tend to display less aggression and
are physically weaker than men. Hence the old Jewish

prayer, 'I thank you God that you did not make me a
Gentile, a slave, or a woman.'

Incidentally, the *bete noire* of sexual comparison in
Christendom is usually identified as the Apostle Paul. His
remarks on women's submission and silence in church
have frequently earned him the reputation of a
misogynist. Not long ago a very devout Christian woman
told me, 'I read my Bible regularly, but I always skip
Paul's letters because he was all wrong about women.'
But more of that later.

The second perspective, **transcendence**, picks up the
threads of Jesus' own example, but denies that in God's
view there is any difference at all between the sexes.
Oddly enough—because transendence and comparison
are almost incompatible—this also takes its cue from
Paul: 'There is neither Jew nor Greek, there is neither
slave nor free, there is neither male nor female; for you
are all one in Christ Jesus' (Gal. 3:28).

Clearly, if transcendence is granted as the fundamental
principle in the relationship of the sexes, a Pandora's box
is opened (or an Aladdin's cave—depending on how you
look at it). A God who refuses to distinguish male and
female would not be predisposed to back an all-male
clergy—a theme we will return to in the next chapter.

Integration, the third perspective, is in a way a resol-
ution of the other two. It is one of the oldest teachings
about marriage in the Judaeo-Christian tradition about
marriage, reiterated by Jesus in Matthew 19:5,6: 'The
two shall become one. So they are no longer two but one.'

What goes into the church as two separate individuals
comes out under a shower of confetti as one—a new
person. Yet once again the principle does not stand on
its own, for the couple emerging from the church door is
unified only in a spiritual and symbolic sense; in all other
respects—except the obvious legal one—they are two
people to whom the idea of oneness may not alone be
helpful in sorting out the question of roles.

How then do these three perspectives fit together? The
clue is in the third one with its reference to Genesis 1

and 2, the oldest divine statements on marriage. Here we find the invitation to frame ordinary human marriage in terms of the Trinity.

Man was created in the image of God and created male and female (Gen. 1:27). Not only that, but woman, made of man's own substance, is reunited with man in marriage—they are of one flesh. Right at the beginning there is suggested to exist in marriage a blending of oneness and separateness of the sort that we in the Christian era have recognized as integral to God Himself.

Two things follow from this. *First*, there is between marriage partners an equivalence of status that may be compared to the co-equality of the Father, Son and Holy Spirit. One does not take precedence over the other through any natural superiority. Whatever has happened since the fall, and whatever distortions of the relationship between the sexes have affected current thinking, the original and archetypal pattern of marriage was exemplified in Genesis. It was a union of two individuals who were spiritual, emotional and intellectual equals.

But, *second*, along with this equivalence of status there went—and must go—a diversity of function. As far as we are able to perceive it, this is true of the Godhead: the Son came into the world to carry out the redemptive plan conceived by the Father, while the Spirit carries the conviction of sin and the gift of salvation. And in this distinction there *does* subsist a sort of precedence, for the Son defers to the Father, and the Spirit, the Comforter, is sent by the Father at the Son's request. It is not forced, not resented; it just exists.

Back to husbands and wives. As a reflection of the Trinity, a marriage confers on man and wife not just an equivalence of status—an idea we now see is hardly modern or the sole property of the feminist lobby!—but also a distinct delineation of roles. A triple diversity in the oneness of God must have its opposite number in the double diversity of the oneness of the marriage. Or, put a bit more simply: one company, different jobs.

But here of course is the big catch. As soon as you put

a dozen equal people together in a company it becomes painfully obvious that the manager is more equal than the rest of them. Function, to some extent or another, inevitably seems to define status.

The human being plus high paying job and big car is a few rungs further up than the human being plus baseball cap and spanner.

Wasn't it precisely this sort of thing that Paul had in mind when in that red hot passage in Ephesians 5 he gave the husband's responsibility in marriage as love, and the wife's as *obedience?* So much for all the fancy talk about equivalent status—when the rubber hits the road it's the same old story of the manacles and the stove!

But if, being a man, you're just about to throw your boots down in the hall, get a drink and flop in front of the TV until your wife cleans up, feeds the kids and makes supper—think again. Love in the Christian vocabulary is no soft option. On a good day it'll demand you think more about other people than about yourself; on a bad day it'll get you crucified.

Nor is it confined to feelings and attitudes. Love isn't thinking warm thoughts about someone or saying mushy things to them. It's cleaning your boots before you take them off, leaving the drink in the fridge, talking to the kids, washing dishes, changing diapers.

Love is not *taking*, as Hollywood implies; rather, it is *giving*, as the Bible teaches. And it's practical! As a husband of fifteen years and father of four, I can testify that it works.

'If a man loves me,' said Jesus, 'he will keep [i.e. obey, submit to] my word. . . . He who does not love me does not keep my words' (John 14:22–24). For futher details turn to 1 Corinthians 13: 'Love is patient, kind, never boastful, arrogant or rude; not irritable or resentful, bearing and enduring all things; it never insists on its own way, never rejoices at wrong, is never jealous. . . .' Maybe you'd prefer to go for the obedience and leave love for the women?

The point is this. If 'love' is a summary statement of a

man's role in marriage, that role demands nothing less than the total sacrifice of himself for the sake of his wife. That is the way of the Cross, what Christian love is all about. And in its way it is a form of submission. When a man loves his wife, as he vows to do in the wedding service, he submits to her by recognizing her needs and seeking only her good.

In effect, although Paul used two separate words to identify the roles of a man and a woman in marriage, they amount in practice to much the same thing—a mutual self-sacrificing love which is the essence of the Trinity.

The principle is exemplified very clearly in the New Testament teaching on marital sex. Neither partner, Paul says in 1 Corinthians 7:3–5, has the right to demand sex or deny it. Why? Because in marriage they own one another's bodies: the self-giving by one partner is so taken for granted that it is expressed as the other's *right*. There is to be no selfishness—if there is then whatever takes place will not be the mutual self-giving love ordained by God. And if abstinence is chosen for a period of time it must be chosen by both man *and* woman.

But love isn't the only item in the Bible's list of male responsibilities. Another, and far more contentious one, is leadership. Genesis doesn't say much about Adam and Eve's respective roles before the fall, but it is certain that Eve's job was to bear the children. That was inherent in her womanhood. Also, she was created as Adam's 'companion'.

A further distinction may be read back into their pre-fallen state from the curses God laid on them afterwards. Not only would Eve now have her pain multiplied in childbearing, but Adam would have to toil to get bread from the ground. He was burdened with hard labour, the boring drudgery with spade and machine, the dispiriting hours spent crammed in a smoky train getting to work—all that goes with the responsibility to provide.

The easy life of Eden was exchanged for one in which the only valid currency was effort and pain. Almost as a matter of necessity roles became more specialized and entrenched. In this context God says to the woman: ' . . . and your desire shall be to your husband, and he shall rule over you' (Gen. 3:16). It was a kind of martial law imposed to cope with mankind's loss of innocence, yet corresponding to the order of God's creation. One of them had to take the lead and be answerable for the mistakes—and it was Adam.

You don't have to watch much TV or read many popular novels before you realize that leadership is among the point scoring features of the ideal male. It is interesting that in a series like *Dynasty* it is presented as desirable also for the female, if at the expense of some of the traditional feminine softness. Leadership of this sort is admirable or intimidating, depending whether you are on the giving or receiving end of it, for it is leadership as *power*.

Consequently, it is the object of intense competition: the Adam of *Dynasty*, Adam Carrington, is not only a leader in his own right (he has to be, or he would not be an appealing character) he is also ambitious for greater leadership, more power. But it is not this desire that makes the viewer hate him, rather the means to which he will stoop to fulfil it—the propriety and desirability of leadership as power is an unspoken assumption.

Defined in the terms of *Dynasty*, God's reservation of leadership to the man would be an outrage. It would not even be good entertainment—which is why leadership in the TV series is fair game for both male and female characters. Who would bother to watch it if Alexis were played by a man and all the women were reduced to spineless, submissive wimps?

For this reason it is impossible to make sense of God's bestowal of leadership on the man without first developing a Christian concept of leadership. And once again here we come back to the paradox of self-giving. He who would be first must be last; he who claims the chief seat must wash everyone else's feet before the meal;

the one who wishes to lead all must daily, hourly be prepared to die for all.

Imagine *that* in *Dynasty*! More to the point, imagine it in the home, for the husband called by God to lead the family is obliged to work out this leadership in humble service. He cleans not just his own boots but everyone else's as well.

And so his wife kicks off her shoes, gets a drink and flops down in front of the TV to watch a football game? Not exactly. Mutual love, mutual service; and in the decision over who does precisely what, a discussion of repective gifts.

The good husband—whose leadership is really a stewardship before God—should as a part of his love for her see that she uses her God-given talents. Maybe she's a real genius at handling money—in that case he may consult her to help out with the family finances. Maybe he fancies himself as a chef—then why not take over some of the cooking?

Marriage involves recognizing, nurturing and expressing each other's abilities, a man and a woman helping each other to be the best they can be, do the best they can do.

This is surely what a woman wants.

To have her full equality affirmed; to have her God-given gifts allowed opportunity to develop and be expressed; to be, with the love of her husband, everything that Christ has called her to be. Neither male leadership nor female submission properly understood should cause offense to her or impinge on what she feels God calling her to. These are part of the coupling, as between two pieces of a jigsaw puzzle, that help to bind a man and a woman together. The two parts are different, but together they make a whole.

And surely that is what a man wants too.

III: WOMEN'S ORDINATION:
Eve at the Altar

I've been spat upon. I've had my life threatened. My family's had their lives threatened. I've been scratched, pushed. I'm a fighter, in the sense that I was willing to do the fighting. It distresses me when I see these people, in some of whom homosexuality plays a part, who are able to shelter their bigotry and fear by forming a line against women. It is fear. That kind of violence stems from fear. I remember seeing a priest take the flesh off a friend's hand as she was giving him communion . . . He tore her hand open on purpose as he took the chalice from her.

(Patricia Stern, Episcopal priest, quoted in the *Guardian*, Nov. 19, 1985)

That men and women in the church of Jesus Christ should have to settle their differences in a manner like this is frankly scandalous. Heated debate is one thing; spitting, assault, and allegations of homosexuality are quite another—as the English say, not exactly cricket. The emotional force behind the issue becomes clear when we realize that in the 1980s women's ordination has effectively split the church down the middle.

In America, the Episcopal church to which Patricia Stern belongs is now almost completely pro. The first women ministers were ordained in 1977, and today only nine out of 102 dioceses refuse to acknowledge them, either because their bishop won't ordain women himself or because he won't confirm their employment in any of his parishes. With the Episcopalians have gone the United Methodist Church, the African Methodist Episcopal Church, the Christian Church, the Presbyterian Church of the USA and the United Church of Christ.

Against women's ordination in the USA are, understandably, the Roman Catholics, along with most Baptist and some Lutheran churches. The Southern Baptist 1984 convention took a stand against the ordaining of women, although owing to denominational structure, the Convention's pronouncements are not binding on individual churches.

In Britain the issue is even hotter. The (Presbyterian) Church of Scotland has been ordaining women for several years. So too have the Baptists, the Methodists and the United Reformed Church. In the Church of England women are still restricted to the office of deaconess, and only in 1985 were they admitted to the diaconate. Opposition to the prospect of women ministering at the altar has produced some strange alliances—notably between the evangelicals and the Anglo-Catholics.

It has also prompted from the Bishop of London the dire prediction of a breakaway, 'true' Church of England forming among the dissidents if the Synod eventually passes the motion. In fact, of the three houses through which legislation has to pass in the Church of England, two—the bishops and the laity—already have sufficient majorities in favour to approve the ordination of women. Significantly perhaps, it is the House of Clergy, the ordinary parish priests, who still oppose it.

Of course the paradox of women's ordination is that while of all the topics treated in this book it is the only one entirely internal to the church, none the less the motive force behind it derives from the general struggle for female equality. You might say that the church, having sowed the seeds of justice and fair play in the society around it, is finally reaping the consequences: the question is justifiably being raised whether Christians who persist in demanding equal treatment for all human beings as children of God should not put their own house in order first.

The suffrage movement took until 1920 to give women the vote in the US, and until 1928 in Britain. Since then, and especially in the last two decades, a lot has changed: by 1982 women numbered 42% of the labor force in America, and probably about the same figure in Britain (the most recent statistic, 39.1%, is for 1975).

But in many areas women are still grossly underrepresented. In both countries women make up a meagre 4% of the national legislature; they still find it hard to compete in top professional jobs and are sometimes openly discriminated against. It is not very surprising then that to the rank and file of the feminist movement an exclusively male clergy appears as an archetypal form of sexist bigotry!

The consequent pressure of public opinion on the church has been enormous, and although there has been an equally wide range of responses these can be distilled down to two basic positions: rejection or accommodation.

Proponents of the first position retreat from any dialogue on the issue and instead take an absolute stand on the teaching of the Bible, which they interpret directly and literally. Paul's remark on women's submission to men (Eph. 5:22) and the impropriety of a woman teaching a man (I Tim. 2:12) are taken at face value. As statements of holy writ they are invested with the same timeless authority as teachings on salvation by faith.

The woman is by the order of creation in a state of submission to the man, and so all the restrictions that follow on this are universally and eternally binding. The woman can no more teach a man today than she could in the congregation to whom Paul addressed his original letter—it is absolutely wrong.

That women cannot and should not lead the church is argued by means of some powerful precedents from the Bible, the whole of which is clearly a patriarchal book. For one, the entire priesthood of the Old Testament was limited to males. God's self-revelation from Genesis to

Revelation is in the masculine, not the feminine gender: male and female *he* created them.

Nowhere in the Old Testament is there the least hint that the writers considered God anything other than a male deity, and when in the New he visited his creation in person he did so in a man's form. Furthermore, the disciples the incarnate God chose to put in charge of his fledgling church were all men. This tradition has been upheld by the church unfailingly for 1900 years and is still upheld by the Roman Catholic Church, which claims a direct line of spiritual descent from Peter himself.

None of these facts is disputed by supporters of the second position. What they do dispute is their *significance*. The second position is able to accommodate women's ordination simply because scriptural injunctions are seen not as absolutes, changeless irrespective of circumstances, but as mediated through culture.

Disentangle the principle of divine teaching from its embodiment in the language and thought forms of the culture through which it was originally expressed, and you are likely to end up with something altogether different. God's will, argue those who take this view, is not locked into the customs and ideas of a bygone age. It is given continuously, and is discovered by distinguishing what is ageless and eternal in the Bible from what is cultural and therefore relative.

A classic example here—and one that most Christians accept unconsciously—is Paul's forbidding women to cut their hair (I Cor. 11:2–16). Taken absolutely, this passage makes hairstyling a pretty straightforward business—no bob, no spikes, no perms. But of course it is generally accepted that the principle behind Paul's instruction was that women in the church should not look like prostitutes. If in his day a prostitute could be recognized by her short hair then the thing to avoid today is not a certain way of wearing the hair, but a certain provocative style of dress and demeanor.

The way the modern church has almost instinctively dropped the prohibition applies to several other matters too. Most women disregard Paul's instructions in II Tim. 2:12 about jewellery and make-up; no minister I have ever met obeys Jesus' command in Mark 6:8 to walk carrying a staff; and as for using unleavened bread for a sacrament, most of us are lucky if at communion we get real bread at all.

These things are easy to accept for most Christians: they are 'common sense'. But the same form of argument can be turned against the great biblical precedents on which rests the weighty defense of male priesthood. So the priests of the Old Testament were men? Does this not signify only the nature of that culture in which the priests operated—a patriarchal culture where many religious ideas, down to the person of God himself, were inevitably expressed in terms of male dominance?

It might be argued that the culture itself was established by God's decree, and therefore that the 'men first' principle was sanctified by God before the culture described him in the language of masculinity. On the other hand we might say—as the supporters of the accommodation position do—that the central issue is that the priest represented men *and* women, and that the fact he was a man was therefore incidental.

The same idea can be applied to Jesus Christ. After all, he had to be a man or a woman—he could not be both—and it is undeniable that social conditions at that time favored his advent as a man. But, it is argued, that does not mean that he did not die for all people irrespective of sex.

At that time his earthly ministry might have suffered by his appearance as a woman, but so far as his priestly capacity is concerned, as representative of the human race, it would be a matter of indifference whether he was a man or a woman. Either way half of those represented would fall on the 'wrong' side of the fence.

If representation is the principle at stake, then, what could be fairer than a clergy made up of women and men?

Nothing fairer, perhaps. None the less, the counter

argument runs, Jesus did have the chance to inaugurate a mixed apostolate and he opted for twelve *men*. This can, of course, be attacked on the same principle: what constituted good strategy for the church 1900 years ago might possibly be unsuitable today.

But it is susceptible to another argument as well, that of consistency. A position that insists on the literal interpretation of scripture must accept all the consequences; the exclusive male priest must be one who also wears his hair short, celebrates with unleavened bread and walks to church staff in hand—a rare creature indeed.

Finally it might be pointed out that when Jesus chose a male apostolate he chose a Jewish male apostolate. Gentiles only became leaders and heirs to apostolic authority with the agreement of the churches at the Council of Jerusalem in Acts 15.

Although the decision of that Council is recorded in the canon of scripture it nevertheless overturns a central tenet of Christian faith and leadership, and stands first in a line of crucial decisions, mostly taken by later councils, which were not covered by that canon. That the ordination of women was not a product of Nicea is arguably an accident of historical circumstance and not the vindication of an eternal law.

In the end, while it is vital to affirm the unchanging nature of God's word, and also to acknowledge how its application has changed, there certainly is such a thing as the continuous revelation of God's will. Sometimes this results in the appearance of ideas previously obscure and unacceptable—as with the preaching to the Gentiles Paul identifies as a mystery hidden until the time of Christ (Eph. 1–3).

It is clear that the twentieth century is the time for the churches to come to one mind on the question of women's ordination. The expansion of women's ministry has resulted in ridiculous anomalies: women often do men's jobs just as well, and in some areas—particularly the mission field—have long enjoyed a numerical advantage. As long ago as 1961 an executive with World Evangelization Crusade (WEC) suggested it should be renamed the Women's Evangelistic Corps. He noted the inherent contradiction in sending women overseas to do the same jobs as men, yet denying them ordination at home.

Where does that leave us? Two further pieces of evidence need to be assembled. First, an analysis of the work women actually did in the early church, and second, another look at the principle of male-female relationships which must govern the question of women's ordination and ministry, whatever view we take of its cultural expression on the Bible.

The early Church carried on in much the same spirit as Jesus began. The evangelist Philip's four daughters all had the gift of prophecy (Acts 21:9) in accordance with the prediction of the prophet Joel quoted by Peter on the first day of Pentecost. Women indeed had been present in the upper room when the Spirit fell (Acts 1:14). The first convert in Europe was a woman—Lydia—and one who, thanks to earlier reforms in Roman law, was successful in business. Luke mentions women as converts in Thessalonica, Berea and Athens, and Paul greets them as fellow workers at the end of his letters to Rome and Philippi (see Acts 17:4, 12, 34: Rom. 16:3,6,12; Phil. 4:2,3).

Unlike the nation of Israel, whose governing body—the Sanhedrin—was for men only, the church found a role for women in leadership. Both John Mark's mother and Nympha had churches meeting in their houses. The couple Priscilla and Aquila, though they are never given a particular title, were clearly held in high esteem by Paul and were instrumental in the conversion of Apollos.

Most important of all Phoebe of Cenchrae—one of the women greeted in Romans 16—is called *diakonos*. This word is rendered in its twenty-one other New Testament occurrences as 'minister' or 'deacon' but here (for reasons that may say more about the translators than the text) simply as 'servant'. If there is any doubt that Phoebe deserves to be placed alongside Stephen and the other fully-accredited deacons of the church it should be

dispelled by the other word used of her here: *prostatis*.
This is a noun seen only once but whose verbal form
appears quite frequently with reference to bishops,
deacons and elders, and is translated 'manage' (cf. I Tim.
3:4,5; Rom. 12:8). Quite how much may be built on this
slender foundation is open to question, but it does at
least suggest that women were given a real role in church
leadership in the days of the New Testament church. As
for the matter of women's ordination— whether and to
what—the precedent of early church practice cannot
settle it, and nor can the hermeneutical arguments of the
'rejectionists' and the 'accommodationists'. Each reveal
a part, but only a part, of the truth: A solid literal
interpretation denies the possibility of progressive revelation: the view that biblical truth is mediated through
culture, though it may show women's leadership to be in
theory consonant with the will of God, cannot prove it
as a fact.

We have to return to the argument of the last chapter.
Here, at least, we were able to come to firm conclusions
on the respective roles of men and women in one social
unit—the family. As with the persons of the Trinity, men
and women are equal in status, but differing in function.
One function that definitely falls on the man's shoulders
is that of leadership.

So far so good. But the principle at work in the structure of the family must logically extend to the larger social
structures of which the family is a constituent part.

What after all is a congregation if not a gathering of
individuals, each of whom are members of a family and
subject to the divine ordering of it? The implications
quickly come clear: A woman cannot be required to exercise a ministry that implies leadership over men, because
men in general are required by scripture to exercise leadership in the home—and more than likely one of the men
in the congregation of a woman minister will be her own
husband!

The suggestion of a celibate clergy for women doesn't
help here. For a start it's unfair—why should male minis-

ters be allowed to marry and female not? But also what applies to one man and one woman in the case of marriage must apply across the board to all men and all women as groups. This, when you have made due allowance for changes in culture, is probably what Paul was getting at in I Tim. 2:12: 'I permit no woman to teach or have authority over men; she is to keep silent.' Silence is hardly a reasonable expectation today! None the less the principle of authority is clearly set out and the terms are collective, not singular: no woman over any man. This is specifically in home and church.

This does not mean women are locked up in the ecclesiastical kitchen. Once again, the Christian interpretation of leadership is extremely demanding of those on whom it is bestowed. The imperatives of self-sacrifice and service apply no less rigorously to men when they're in the pulpit than when they're at home. In fact their conduct in either place should give no woman cause to think herself suppressed or restricted. On the contrary there is ample scope for what we might call supplementary women's leadership, as deacons, members of the board of trustees or committees, and over the part of the church congregation made up of other women—which in most churches is far more than fifty percent. The only tree in the garden whose fruit may not be picked is that of spiritual authority. Beyond that single caveat there should be the same creative sharing of work between the sexes at church as there can be in the home.

IV: DIVORCE: Untying the Knot

Nowhere is the church's attitude toward moral issues more schizophrenic than in its treatment of divorce.

Take the case of a friend of mine in southern California. Abandoned by his wife, he approached his evangelical pastor for some comfort and advice. They talked for some time, and finally the pastor said to him, 'Well, if divorce is what you both want, then that's okay.' Then he added with a smile, 'But if you divorce, both of you will have to join the singles' class.'

The remark was probably made with the best of intentions; after all, for someone in the throes of emotional trauma, humor may come as a welcome relief. But to my friend it was devastating; he had come to the church expecting firmness and gravity—qualities traditional in any clergyman's consideration of divorce—and instead he had received open-ended advice delivered in a manner little short of flippant. Why?

The answer is obvious enough when you realize modern western society runs precisely on these lines. Morality is open-ended, and morality that is open-ended will not long keep flippancy at bay. A marriage entered into without conditions or commitments is almost by definition something not to be taken seriously; it is easily made and just as easily unmade. And if the unmaking causes a certain amount of stress and sorrow, that is all part of the game: you pick yourself up, dust yourself off and get set for the next round. It's back to the singles' class till the next match.

Of course it may be asked: What business does the *church* have propounding such a view? My friend in California would have found the pastor's remarks a good deal less offensive if they'd come from someone outside the congregation.

That someone inside the church should treat divorce lightly is a measure of the contamination of the church by modern secular values. Once again the initiative is passing in the wrong direction; instead of leading, the church is allowing itself to be led.

As has been said by the Rev. Daniel Sullivan, rector of a large Episcopal parish in Pennsylvania: 'The church keeps on adjusting its canon law and church discipline to accommodate the pressure of society in the area of divorce instead of investing money and efforts in supporting the family unit and family life.'

The question of the morality of divorce is not new: in fact it was raised directly by the Pharisees in the New Testament. 'And Pharisees came up to him and tested him by asking, "Is it lawful to divorce one's wife for any cause?" ' (Matt. 19:3). The question was asked—and answered—in a specific cultural context, and certain specific issues (relating to the interpretation of the Old Testament) were at stake. Naturally the Pharisees were trying to catch Jesus. But at the root of the thing lay a social paradox: the simultaneous sanctity of marriage and ease of divorce.

Jewish culture in general had a very high view of marriage. So much a sacred duty was it that the man who reached his twenty-first birthday without a bride was considered to be breaking the positive command of God to be fruitful and multiply. And multiplying was the name of the game, with heavy reprimands for the loser. As the proverb solemnly declared, 'He who has no children slays his own posterity.'

The childless man—unless exempted by the study of the Law from all marital responsibility—sinned by lessening the image of God on the earth. Built into this were important safeguards for the women: rape and adultery were punishable by death and, in the case of a bride accused of impurity, the onus lay on the husband to prove his charge. In short, if a woman obeyed the moral standards enjoined upon her by the Law—if she avoided adultery and prostitution—then because of the general priority given to childraising her position was secure.

Or almost secure.

The trouble was, in a patriarchal and polygamous society such as that of Israel in the Old Testament, women came to be treated as a sort of capital stock. A man could take as many wives as he had means to support, and very often the number he took was a measure of his wealth.

But if there was no prohibition against the accumulation of wives, neither was there any against their removal. The man wishing to divorce his wife had only to commit his intentions to paper, and the job was done—hardly what you'd call bureaucratic red tape. Take this passage from Deuteronomy which though technically about remarriage is the only one in the Law to deal with divorce:

> When a man takes a wife and marries her, if then she finds no favour in his eyes because he has found some indecency in her, and he writes her a bill of divorce and puts it in her hand and sends her out of his house, and if she goes and becomes another man's wife, and the latter husband dislikes her and writes a bill of divorce . . . or if the latter husband dies . . . then the former husband, who sent her away, may not take her again to be his wife . . . (Deut. 24:1–4)

The woman had no say in the matter, no legal rights. She could not initiate divorce herself even in the direst situation. But the moment the husband wished to divorce *her* the matter could be over within minutes—easier than firing an employee.

Now for the sixty-four thousand dollar question.

Rough as it was on the woman the Law had not left

her helpless, for it assumed a divorce must have legitimate grounds. But what were those grounds? What actually constitutes the 'some indecency' cryptically referred to by Moses in Deuteronomy 24?

By the time of Christ opinions had polarized in two camps.

The more liberal view, propounded by rabbis of the school of Hillel, considered the indecency to cover everything down to the most trivial misdemeanors. A woman risked divorce if she talked to other men in public or burned her husband's dinner.

According to the school of Shammai, on the other hand, legitimate grounds for divorce meant adultery and nothing else. This was a far stricter ruling and far less convenient for a male-dominated society, which understandably favoured Hillel's version. Eventually this society made divorce not only an option, but compulsory if a woman proved either unfaithful or sterile.

Theologically speaking, then, in Jesus' day the matter of culpable indecency was a hot issue. The arguments were well-worn and familiar, and all anyone had to do to register his opinion on it was vote for or against the motion. But of course there was more to it than that, because 'voting' at all carried a strong implication of party allegiance: you showed what colour of badge was hidden beneath your lapel. This was a good enough reason for the Pharisees to put the question to Jesus, who always claimed to have no badges at all. 'Is it lawful to divorce one's wife for any cause?'

Theology, like politics, tends to major on things about which people disagree.

Supporters of Hillel and Shammai—like Republicans and Democrats, Socialists and Tories, Episcopalians and Presbyterians—would have been acutely aware of the things that divided them. But in fact, like many opposing parties, they also had much in common—specifically a high regard for the authority of God's word in scripture. It is on this common ground that Jesus builds his reply. No Jew, after all, would have quibbled with the creation story, and you can hardly cite an earlier, more categorical precedent on divorce than what God said about the nature of marriage in Genesis. So Jesus simply quotes it:

> Have you not heard that he who made them from the beginning made them male and female, and said, 'For this reason a man shall leave his father and mother and be joined to his wife, and they two shall become one flesh'? So they are no longer two but one flesh. What therefore God has joined together, let not man put asunder. (Matt. 19:4–6)

Briefly, in God's first plan there was no room for divorce on any grounds. The sinless Adam and Eve could no more be divorced than the egg could be removed from a fruitcake—the very idea was nonsense. The ruling then is uncompromising and absolute.

But like any absolute ruling it is open to the test of consistency: it's no good dad saying 'no ice creams' when mom is already up at the counter buying them. And it is this point that the Pharisees are quick to pick up: 'Why then did Moses command one to give a certificate of divorce, and put her away?' (Matt. 19:7).

The key phrase in Jesus' reply to this is 'for your hardness of heart'. Only because of that did Moses allow divorce; otherwise the Law would stand as God originally intended. Divorce finds a place in the Law not as a statement of God's will, but as a *concession* to weak and perverted human nature. It is a means of containing human sin and misery.

But, says Jesus, 'from the beginning it was not so; And I say to you: whoever divorces his wife, except for unchastity, and marries another, commits adultery' (Matt. 19:8,9). Here is Shammai's position restated in a stronger form. This is no reasoned interpretation of the Law—a thing the Pharisees excelled in—but a direct appeal to God's own, incontrovertible command. Divorce only because human sin destroys a relationship from

within before it is formally dissolved. Divorce, in other
words, only for adultery.

This standpoint has been developed further in Christian
teaching. One further concession is added in the New
Testament, by Paul: 'If the unbelieving partner desires to
separate, let it be so; in such a case a brother or sister is
not bound' (I Cor. 7:15). It is Paul also who compares
marriage to the love of Christ for his church: there is
one Saviour, one church, one mutual self-sacrificing love
based on commitment of will.

Some parts of the church have viewed marriage with
such reverence that they have elevated it to the status of
a sacrament. If it is not strictly 'an outward and visible
sign of an inward and spiritual grace' nor specifically
'ordered by Christ himself' (to quote from the definition
in the Anglican Prayer Book) it is certainly a high calling
undertaken soberly and with the expectation of
permanence.

In a way the polarity still exists between this conservative view and the widespread liberal one in the tradition
of Hillel. Marriage in the west is frequently based on
feelings of romance or sexual attraction, and maintained
through a sense of duty or social propriety; increasingly
it is not maintained at all. Divorce, and what Alvin Toffler
fifteen years ago called serial marriage, are becoming the
norm and not the exception. The difference between the
modern situation and the ancient one where Hillel's ideas
were practised is that the indecency providing grounds
for divorce now applies to men as well as women, and
can, in the case of a *nolo contendere* divorce, be agreed
by mutual consent.

If the church is not going to go along with this moral
drift we should ask what alternative is left to us. A church
not only feels the pressure of outside public opinion; it
has to deal with the effect that changing social ideas have
on its members. The pastor who gives a talk to high
school students on the moral status of divorce may well
return to his office to find himself counseling a couple in
his own congregation whose marriage is on the verge of

breakdown. Practical as well as theoretical answers are needed.

A good illustration of this is the tendency Christians sometimes have of standing in moral judgment on people who do things they disagree with. Take the case of a woman who came to me recently in deep distress because her elder sister—of whom she had always been envious—had just gone through a divorce. 'I let her know that my marriage was secure,' she said, 'and that I would hold my marriage together, no matter what.' This in itself is interesting; why should she need to comment about her *own* marriage in the face of her sister's divorce?

But that wasn't all.

The crisis came when, kneeling at the altar rail to receive communion, she saw her sister coming to receive on the other side. Her sister—a divorcee, a sinner. Now this is a single case, but it speaks volumes about the psychological position of a certain part of the Christian community: the insecurity, the shoring up of defenses, the closing of ranks against moral contamination, the emphasis, presented with a moral challenge, on *condemnation*.

Christians who have suffered marital breakdown themselves sometimes gain a different perspective on things. One man who had been through a divorce the previous year told me that his wife had been having an affair. This of course is one of the few instances where divorce is actually condoned in the Bible; he had the right to carry through a divorce and do it with a clear conscience. And yet he had been unable to reconcile the biblical pattern with his own state of mind. 'I was unfaithful in hundreds of ways,' he said, 'long before she ever went into the arms of another man.'

In fact he was not the mistreated innocent implied in the biblical model, and probably no one is. There is only innocence, and guilt, by degree. It takes two to make a marriage and it takes two to break it. If we're going to talk about condemnation we'd better take down our glass houses pretty quick before someone else picks up the first

stone. It doesn't matter whether we're the injured party
or just onlookers—there's a little bit of the wicked witch
in all of us.

But then there's a bit of the victim in all of us too. I've
met many divorced people over the years, and have often
asked them what they learned from their experience.
'How selfish I was,' say some of them, or, 'I married
because I thought it was the right thing to do at eighteen.'
'I learned that it's easy to talk about marriage,' say others,
'but living with another person every day takes a level of
commitment and maturity I didn't know anything
about. . . .'

All of them have suffered, been scarred, and felt a
deep sense of failure in spite of the casual attitude society
takes to divorce. It is this sense of brokenness that needs
to be recognized in the church; it is a brokenness like any
other kind—a conviction of failure that invites
compassion, forgiveness, new beginnings. This is not to
obscure the contradiction between divorce and the perfect
will of the Creator, only to acknowledge it as integral to
the frailty of a fallen human race. It was to the woman
taken in adultery—caught in the betrayal of her marriage
vows—that Christ said, 'Your sins are forgiven. Go, and
sin no more.'

I never finished the story of the woman and her sister
at the altar rail. It goes on, in her own words, like this:

Then it seemed as if God spoke to me. For the first
time in my life, I saw myself like the Pharisee in the
parable Jesus told. As I knelt there, waiting for my
priest to give me the sacrament, it felt as if I had been
telling the Lord how good I was and how fortunate he
was to have me for his daughter. My sister knelt on
the far side of the altar, away from the others, ashamed
and guilt ridden. If Jesus Christ had spoken in an
audible voice would he have said that one sister went
from the church justified and forgiven? If he had, it
would have been my sister he meant.

I would argue that this concept of forgiveness is at least as central to the Christian faith as the judgement of sin. The church can say quite clearly that divorce is wrong, is against the perfect will of God, without turning it into a spiritual shibboleth. At the same time it can recognize brokenness, tragedy, and need of forgiveness without opening the gates to moral relativism and divorce on demand.

In a fallen universe the 'right' way is not always a blameless one, but the least blameworthy: the lesser of two evils. The Pharisees, who after all were masters in the art of Sabbatarianism, did not hesitate to break the Sabbath by pulling a mule from the ditch, and Christ himself, the master of the Sabbath, again and again sacrificed its observance on the altar of compassion. If we counsel a loving firmness on the issue of divorce we will be in good company, following a pattern laid down not only by Christ but by Christians throughout history, among them Luther, Calvin, Knox and Wesley. They seemed to reach a sensible working formula on its application:

The Reformers . . . . did recognize certain legitimate grounds for divorce and remarriage, such as adultery, desertion and cruelty. These grounds were legitimate, however, only as so judged by the church or corporate body. . . . To put it differently, the Reformers saw that man was not necessarily made for marriage, but that marriage was made for man.

(Stanley A. Ellisen, *Divorce and Remarriage in the Church*, Zondervan, 1977)

V: HOMOSEXUALITY: ADAM and stEVE

Some time in the early 1970s 'gay' became chic.

It had been theoretically chic for a while, with the removal of homosexuality from the American Psychiatric Association's list of mental disorders, the legal authorization of homosexual acts between consenting adults (1961 in the first American state, Illinois, and 1967 in Britain), and, most important, with the 1942 Kinsey Report, *Sexual Behavior in the Human Male*.

The Kinsey report was crucial because it established a scientific rationale for homosexuality. No less than 25% of American males, it asserted, had had some homosexual experience, while 4% of them were exclusively gay. Furthermore, this could be explained quite naturally by the fact that—in the opinion of the report's authors—every individual's sexual orientation lay not at one of two opposite points, but somewhere along a continuum between the two. Far from committing a felony, the man with a strongly feminine character who chose to live with another male was now making a realistic expression of his sexuality.

The ball was finally set rolling at 3 a.m. on June 28th 1969. A police raid on the Stonewall Inn in Greenwich Village, New York, caused a forty minute riot by two hundred gays, later followed by a series of protest rallies. Militant gay activism had been born, and in far-away places foundations began to shake.

How little notice the Christian church had taken of gay rights is indicated by the issue with reference to which homosexuality was most decisively challenged—not gay morality in general or even Christian gay morality, but whether or not gays should be *ordained*. Even so, arguments were soon overtaken by events. The task force set up by the United Presbyterian Church of the USA in 1976 was still at work when the first homosexual, Ellen Marie Barrett—gay rights advocate and practising lesbian—was ordained to the Episcopalian priesthood by the Bishop of New York.

The result? A split. While homosexual practice does not receive general approval, what might be called the gay *image*, with its emphasis on snappy dressing and avant-garde ideas, is at least sufficiently acceptable to be represented on *Dynasty*—which, given the stakes in the ratings war, is no mean achievement.

Similarly with the church. The Presbyterian task force, perhaps conscious of the church's public image, came down in favor of homosexual practice in certain circumstances. This view was rejected first by some members of the task force itself—who filed their own minority report—and then by the General Assembly. After disallowing the ordination of gays, the Assembly voted twelve to one in favor of a motion condemning gay behavior.

Britain has shown the same tendency towards polarization. In 1979 a working party commissioned by the Church of England's Board of Social Responsibility published its findings under two headings, *Report* and *Critical Observations*. These critical observations represented the same conservative stance taken by the Presbyterian Assembly. Although the report as a whole was fairly moderate, there none the less followed a swift and strong reaction from the Evangelical wing of the church.

This sort of response—from Christians who think that homosexual behavior is, when all is said and done, clearly a sin—is typically condemned by the gay rights movement as pig-headed and intolerant. That is a powerful card to play; no one in the 1980s likes to be dubbed intolerant, especially as regards minority groups. Tolerance is integral to freedom and as Lincoln himself insisted, you can't have one without the other. Freedom means freedom for the slave as well as the settler, whether or not you like the color of his skin.

Taken to its logical conclusion this argument demands our patient sufferance of rapists, assassins, child-molesters and every imaginable deviant. But this clearly isn't how our society handles its less public-minded members. Somewhere along the line a distinction is drawn—has to be drawn—between those whose freedom may be indulged, and those from whom it must be removed until they can use it for the good of society as a whole.

Tolerance, in other words, is not unconditional: it is bound by a legal code that limits the damage one individual may, by exercising his freedom, inflict on another. What is tolerated is what is generally agreed to be *harmless*.

Now that is all well and good until you realize that harmlessness itself has no fixed definition and that the number of behavior patterns to which the word has become attached has grown rapidly since the fifties. In a lot of cases, of course, the label is justified. Few will seriously contend that fashions in hair and clothing in themselves destroy the moral fabric of society. But along with these changes have gone other ones—permissive attitudes toward sex, violence on the media, the gay lifestyle—all accepted as harmless and in some cases justified as honest or helpful in personality development.

Furthermore, all this goes on under the slogan of liberation, an emotive term to say the least since the various social and legal restraints from which a particular type of behavior has to be liberated are automatically cast in the role of oppressor. The word liberation, most would agree, is aptly applied to the emancipation of slaves and inaptly applied to the legalization of crime.

But between these two extremes lie a horde of muddy ethical questions in which the lifting of restrictions may or may not be a liberation. At this point, people who feel there are good reasons for keeping restrictions in place will become angry at those who pre-empt the argument by using a terminology which implies strongly and subtly that restrictions are, *a priori*, a bad thing.

This is a reasonable summary of the situation with Gay Lib and its Christian opponents.

Christianity is not—or should not be—a reactionary force. Its moral code does not preclude development, dialogue or the consideration of new ideas. But for Christianity that takes its cue from biblical teaching there is always a bottom line on moral issues. Once that is reached, the church is obliged to stick to it. That is part of moral leadership.

The early Christians would face the lions' pit before conceding what to many would have seemed a fine theological distinction between one and several gods. So today, when a Christian father refuses to let his children be taught by gays, he is not practising bigotry, narrow-mindedness or intolerance but asserting a rational view based on argument and biblical precedents his conscience cannot avoid.

That is a hard stand to make. It's putting your feet in the stocks and taking all the rotten tomatoes society can throw at you. That is why many official church bodies required to look into the issue have played it safe and compromised.

When one gay rights advocate said of the biblical injunctions against homosexuality 'If you really understand the Bible properly it does not teach that at all: the New Testament, especially, teaches a God who loves everyone', he was pressing for a concession many Christians have been only too willing to make. Theirs is a tolerant twentieth century God, for whom love covers a multitude of sins. For this reason any treatment of the church's position on gay rights must begin with the biblical case, and that traditionally begins with Sodom and Gomorrah.

The story is well known. Hearing that Lot has received visitors the residents of Sodom gathered round his house and demanded that he send them out, 'that we may know them' (Gen. 19:5). Contrary to the opinion of some commentators the Sodomites weren't out to display their civic-mindedness; the Hebrew word translated 'know'—*yadha*—does mean know in the modern sense, but it also carries overtones of carnal knowledge, and is used this way ten times in the Old Testament. 'Now Adam *knew* Eve his wife,' says Gen. 4:1, 'and she conceived, and bore Cain. . . .'

That Lot refused the Sodomites' demand and offered as a substitute to send out his two daughters who 'have not known men' (vs. 9), and that the Sodomites in return decided to storm the house, suggests this is the meaning intended here. Consequently they were struck blind, and after Lot and his family had got away from the city, 'The Lord rained on Sodom and Gomorrah brimstone and fire from the Lord out of heaven' (vs. 24).

Of course the story doesn't include a list of the specific actions by which the Sodomites brought down the judgment of God, but that homosexual intercourse was one of them has been agreed by nearly all commentators, Jewish and Christian, since it was first set down.

Incidentally it is often remarked by modern critics that Lot could have done better than shove his two virgin daughters out to receive whatever indignities were in store for his guests. This is true; but it should also be pointed out that in the moral code of the day hospitality was a sacred vow to be honored if necessary with the lives of the hosts. In the same moral code it unfortunately fell to the women to honor it first.

A similar story, though with a different ending, is related in Judges 19. Here the visitors are an Ephraimite and his wife, a concubine, who break a long journey by staying overnight with another Ephraimite living in Gibea, a town in Benjaminite territory. In the evening the building is surrounded by a band of men.

The translators of the New English Bible are in no doubt as to their intentions: 'Bring out the man who has gone into your house, for us to have intercourse with him' (19:22). Once again the verb is *yadha;* once again the host offers his virgin daughter as a substitute. When the men refuse to accept her the visiting Ephraimite pushes his concubine out of the door to be abused and eventually killed. Unable the next morning to gain any justice from the authorities, he cuts her body into pieces and sends a portion to each of the other eleven tribes, thus precipitating a holy war.

In both the above cases the evidence against homosexual intercourse is circumstantial—it is deduced from the actions of the men involved and the judgments of God upon them. But in the Holiness Code of Leviticus 18–20 the matter is spelled out in black and white. Here God builds into the Law of Israel specific prohibitions against the misuse of sex: intercourse during menstruation, adultery, temple prostitution, bestiality—and homosexual intercourse. 'And you shall not lie with a male as with a woman; it is an abomination . . . If a man lies with a male as with a woman, both of them have committed an abomination; they shall be put to death, their blood is upon them' (Lev. 18:22; 20:13).

This might seem to be the end of the matter, but an ingenious argument has been raised in the interpretation of Leviticus by a theologian who as a gay has an interest in showing the legitimacy of homosexual acts. His point is that *to'ebah*, translated abomination, refers to that which is ritually unclean, and not to intrinsic evil. The eating of pork, for instance, is *to'ebah*. It cannot be wrong in itself or it would still be outlawed in the New Testament; it is included in the prohibitions of Leviticus because it causes *ritual* impurity—something which under the new covenant concerns us little if at all. Further, he argues, the inclusion of homosexuality in the prohibitions may have come about simply because of its association with the old Canaanite practices of temple prostitution and child sacrifice. In other words, it was prohibited not because it was wrong in itself, but because it was Canaanite and therefore liable to seduce men into idol worship.

This argument is flawed on two counts. First, though

the meaning of the word *to'ebah* is wide enough to include quite trivial things (like the Egyptians' dislike of foreigners) it also covers offenses hard to dismiss as mere ritual impurity. False scales, described as *to'ebah* in Proverbs 11:1 might have caused their user to be ritually unclean, but they also made him a dishonest swindler. Similarly the sacrificial burning of children must have been, as well as a ritual offense, a contravention of the sixth commandment.

To prove a thing ritually impure is not to prove it morally right; rather the opposite is implied. At the very least, the onus is on the gay theologians to show that homosexual behavior isn't intrinsically as well as ritually wrong. Here the argument must fail because in the Bible it's hard to find a good word spoken of it.

This second point is fatal to all attempts to justify homosexuality from the scripture, even the one that defines perversion as the commission of homosexual acts by heterosexuals. This argument further claims that the Bible is silent about those whose homosexual behavior is a sincere, loving and natural expression of a homosexual nature—carried on in relationships as enduring and stable as traditional Christian marriage.

To base your entire moral system on an argument from silence is, to put it kindly, unwise. It is at least as reasonable to suggest that if God had meant to approve gay sexuality he would have said so. The world of the New Testament after all gave him ample scope.

But no.

In his letter to the church in that most licentious of Greek cities, Corinth, Paul lists homosexuality along with greed, drunkenness, idolatry, adultery and theft as the traits of those whose unrighteousness will prevent their inheriting the kingdom of God. (See 1 Cor., 6:9–11). The list is extended in I Timothy: the ungodly and sinners, the unholy and profane, murderers of mothers, manslayers, sodomites, kidnappers, liars, perjurers, and (for good measure) agents of whatever else is contrary to sound doctrine (1:8–11).

All this is without reference to any distinction between ritual and intrinsic wrong. For Paul homosexual behavior is always the same nasty corruption of the way it ought to be:

> For this reason God gave them up to dishonorable passions. Their women exchanged natural relations for unnatural, and the men likewise gave up natural relations with women and were consumed with passion for one another, men committing shameless acts with men and receiving in their own persons the due penalty for their error. (Rom. 1:26,27)

Nor is Paul the only New Testament writer with strong words to say about homosexuality, though other references are indirect. Jude for instance, uses the Greek term *hetera sarx*, rendered 'other flesh', or 'unnatural lust'. The angels were damned for their sexual relations with humans, he says, 'just as Sodom and Gomorrah and the surrounding cities, which likewise acted immorally and indulged in unnatural lust, served as an example by undergoing an eternal punishment' (Jude 7,8).

The likely explanation for the euphemism is the habit of the later prophets of avoiding any specific mention of the sin of sodomy; but the implication is clear, as is the endorsement of its condemnation. Peter, treating the same issue in his second epistle, uses almost every alternative expression: 'the licentiousness of the wicked', 'the immoral conduct of lawless men', those who 'indulge in the lust of defiling passion' and 'filthy bodily lust'.

There is one last part of the Bible cited unfailingly by those who wish to prove homosexuality is a Christian option—the story of David and Jonathan. The 'purple passage' appears in II Sam. 1:26, when Jonathan has been killed by the Philistines and David looks back sadly on their friendship: 'I grieve for you, Jonathan, my brother; dear and delightful you were to me; your love for me was wonderful, surpassing the love of women.'

The gay interpretation of this verse insists that the love
surpassing that of women must necessarily be sexual in
nature and erotic in expression. But again the argument
is from silence: if David and Jonathan *did* have a homosexual affair then the details furnishing conclusive proof
have been omitted from the tale. Why? Perhaps the
scribe, wishing to make David more appealing to a later
generation, deliberately left them out.

But then inconsistencies would have arisen. David, for
instance, would not be presented as he is—a paragon of
virtue, courage, and obedience—if he had spent a good
part of his life engaged in open or clandestine homosexuality explicitly condemned by the Law. In fact, had he
broken the Law in this way (and remember, sodomy was
a capital offense in Israel) we would not expect to find
him paying such meticulous attention to the rest. A man
willing to risk his neck committing sodomy with the king's
son would hardly pass up the opportunity to kill the king,
an unpredictable old man, just because he was the Lord's
anointed.

On top of all that, both he and Jonathan were husbands
and fathers; if David had a fault it was an overdeveloped
taste for women, not weakness for men. His affair with
Bathsheba is explained, in effect, as consequent upon his
standing around on the palace roof spying in other
people's bedrooms.

The other and simpler explanation for the lack of proof
is that such proof never existed.

There is a tendency today to see romantic love as the
crown prince of human emotions, unparalleled in depth
and for which all other loves must be forsaken. But this
is not true in any general sense. David's compliment to
Jonathan that his love surpassed the love of women is
most likely to mean that his faithful companionship was
of greater value than the attentions of a wife—especially
when we bear in mind that 'the love of women' in the
ancient world was usually limited to giving sexual fulfilment and bearing children.

The presence of *eros* in that surpassing love is not only

inconsistent with the historical and religious context, it is a hypothesis that could probably only have arisen in the twentieth century West—with its chronic cynicism and penchant for reading into every possible situation its own peculiar system of sexual values.

The upshot of all this is that there is no such thing as a Christian gay—at least not Christian in the sense of standing under and obeying the word of God, and not gay in the sense that homosexual urges are indulged in practice.

But we are of course assuming that homosexuality is a matter of choice, much like drunken driving or theft. This is a notion rejected by all gays inside or outside the church. In their view homosexuality is a predisposition, caused either by genetic factors or a combination of genetic factors and preconscious 'imprinting' during the first five years of life. Both leave a mark on the personality as indelible as a scar or birthmark on the body: the person did not choose to be gay, and he cannot therefore be held morally responsible for his gay inclinations.

Right away, then, homosexuality is placed on a par with sex and race as a characteristic outside the scope of moral choice. You might condemn a woman who is guilty of fraud or shop-lifting, but you cannot condemn her because she is a *woman*. Nor, the argument goes, can you condemn her for doing the things for which her sexuality predisposes her—falling in love with a man, menstruating, having children. Who is going to condemn gays, then, for doing what their personalities incline them to do?

There are several points to be made in reply to this.

To start with, it is certainly true that environmental factors—childhood, a male school, prison—can incline a person towards homosexuality, and it may be true (though it has not been proved) that homosexuality can be a genetic trait. But this in itself has no moral significance: the Bible implicitly draws the same distinction as the gays between disposition and action. Homosexuality as a disposition is no more or less remarkable than the disposition all men and women have to act outside God's will—we call it Original Sin.

It is when a disposition (whether it be to drink, lying, anger or whatever) is given *expression* in thoughts or words or actions that a person becomes morally culpable. But, as the homosexual will be quick to point out, this is to assume homosexuality as a disposition may be included under Original Sin, that (to return to an earlier place in the discussion) it is not harmless and therefore not to be tolerated. To which the Christian replies—yes. He may or may not be able to see a reason for it, but if in the end homosexual behavior is wrong because the Bible says it's wrong and the Bible is the final arbiter, he has no choice but to abide by its decision.

This might seem to be terribly unfair to the homosexual. But then it is also true that the Bible does not make the same rigid connection as the gays do between homosexual inclinations and homosexual behavior. The whole thrust of the gospel is that while we must call a sin a sin, we will if we want to have the power to resist temptation.

Even gays themselves admit the possibility of this, albeit unwittingly; it is present in the very arguments they use to justify homosexuality. If homosexuality does result from imprinting, as some of them argue, there is at least in theory the option of consulting a psychiatrist whose business it is to help correct and counter aberrant behavior patterns!

And if it is genetic it is still no more irresistible than alcoholism. Any member of Alcoholics Anonymous will tell you that while he is by nature an alcoholic, with the support of the group he can stay dry.

This is not to say that being 'straight' will be easy or painless for someone whose homosexual inclinations are very strong, but it does endorse what many reformed gays themselves testify—that the bridge linking disposition to action is crossed by conscious exertion of the will:

Whatever happens is not accidental; gayness is a deliberate decision, though not often a rational one.

True, children have no choice regarding family set-up,
so they may not be responsible for being gay. They are
accountable for what they do with their lives, however,
especially when other people are affected. It's a hard
thing to admit, but somewhere along the line, every
homosexual has chosen to conform his behavior to his
desires. The gay churches seek to elevate this painful
choice to a respectable level.

(*Gayness is upon us*, researched by Jim Kaspar,
Daily Planet Publications, 1974)

The Bible pays no special attention to homosexuality over
and above any other sin; it is one among many, to which
people are susceptible in varying degrees, and from which
anyone can be set free if he or she so wishes. This is the
impartial benefit of the gospel.

But that is not the way it comes across to the gay
community. Partly because our society is embarrassed
and obsessive about sex anyway—and partly because a
special stigma attaches itself to sexual perversions and
the moral case against them is so clear cut—there is a
temptation to treat homosexual behavior and homosexuals themselves with self-conscious caution, and sometimes with outright hostility. Presumably it is this plague
mentality that led the gay community to nickname the
AIDS epidemic Falwell's Revenge.

But it is at the personal level too that we handle gays
with the social forceps. For example one homosexual
once said to me: 'If I stood up in any church and asked
for prayer for help with my homosexuality, people would
regard me with disgust.' He had once confessed his
problem in a support group of Christians. 'You should
have seen the reaction. Instead of the hearty handshake
or embrace I normally received from them when we left,
they avoided touching me. When I went to church the
following Sunday, none of them did more than give me
a quick greeting and got as far away from me as possible.

Naturally, I never returned to that church again and I've never been able to talk to a group about my problem . . .'

If one wing of the church has erred by over-emphasising God's love and thus failing to discriminate between right and wrong, the other wing has allowed love to be swallowed by its moral judgments.

Together they are the priest and Levite who seeing the injured man (in this modern rendering of the parable, the homosexual) walk by on the other side—one because his theology will not allow him to believe the man is in any real trouble, the other because he feels that if the man *is* in trouble it's his own fault and he doesn't deserve any help until he starts making an effort himself.

As with our approach to divorce there must be *compassion* if Christian faith is to be real and convincing. The biblical judgment on homosexual activity as sin must be uncompromisingly maintained, and this will mean among other things that active homosexuals must be excluded from the clergy just as any other person indulging in conscious sin should be excluded. But at the same time we must remember this sin is not especially gross. The gay fighting his homosexual inclinations is just a man or woman grappling with his or her particular weakness, and we all have some weakness, be it anger, greed or heterosexual lust. In this sense the repentant gay is not a moral freak; he is on a par with the rest of us—a brother in arms.

VI: ABORTION: Murder on Demand?

A favorite little story told by anti-abortionists is this one. There was once a family. The father was syphilitic, the mother tubercular. None the less they insisted on having children and quickly produced a whole brood of invalids: one blind, one mute, one with his mother's tuberculosis. One died at birth. When the mother became pregnant a fifth time many modern gynaecologists would have told her to quit and have the child aborted. But there were no gynaecologists, no ready means of abortion, so in nine months the child was born. They took him to church to have him christened. The name—Ludvig van Beethoven.

Abortion has been around for a long time. It seems to have been practised widely in both Greece and Rome—though, as you might expect, more widely among the rich than the poor—and to have survived at least until the age of Augustine. But if abortion was common so, too, were measures restricting its use. There is some evidence for an anti-abortion law having existed in the Greek world; and the famous Hippocratic Oath, even if we have no proof of it originated with Hippocrates or was adhered to by those after him, did include a specific reference to abortion:

. . . neither will I administer a poison to anybody when asked to do so, not will I suggest such a course. Similarly, I will not give to a woman a pessary to cause abortion.

The philosophers seem to have had fewer scruples. Plato in his *Republic* advocates abortion for women who conceive over the age of forty, and in certain circumstances allows not only abortion but infanticide. This practice of exposing an infant—abandoning him with the intention of causing death—is also recommended in Aristotle's *Politics*, along with compulsory abortion where pregnancy threatens to tip family size over the ideal limit.

This was utilitarian approach to abortion. The welfare of the innocent individual was subordinate to that of the state, to the extent of the former being sacrificed for the latter should it be deemed expedient.

Of course this is not the same as abortion on demand: simply the practical expression of certain political principles. Nor did Plato or Aristotle ever put their theories to the test in the real world. When it came to practicalities the greater good was usually agreed to lie not in more abortions but in fewer. This point was conceded in the first century AD even by the Stoics. Their opinion was that until its first breath, the infant was simply a part of the mother; therefore, abortion was morally equivalent to an appendectomy.

Rome, of course, was a utilitarian society *par excellence* in a way that Greece had never been. Weakness was not to be tolerated in her citizens any more than in the stones that held up her mighty bridges and viaducts, and to be branded as weak you had only to be deformed or female. The Roman father who exposed an infant because it was not a son would have had the legal backing of the earliest Roman law code, the Twelve Tables, dated around 450 BC—and presumably the full approval of his neighbors. But he would also have had less incentive to order an abortion, since his concern was not with the pregnancy as such but that the 'product' should be satisfactory.

As the republic gave way to the empire this early leniency began to be challenged. Cicero (d. 43 BC) called for deliberate abortion to be made a capital offence and, when Octavian became Caesar Augustus in 27 BC, abortion was among the items on his list of legal reforms.

But for two reasons reforms had little lasting effect. First, the brunt of moral indignation, such as it was, was borne not by abortion but by infanticide—an act the public could more readily associate with murder. And second, as time went on abortion came to be seen as it is today, as a useful alternative to contraception. This was consequent on developments in medicine in general:

> Great advances in medicine contributed to this phenomenon. Gynaecology developed as a science. There were many woman physicians, some of whom wrote handbooks on abortion which were read by rich women and prostitutes. Both mechanical and chemical contraception were practised; when contraception failed, abortion could be performed in many ways.
> (Michael Gorman, *Abortion and the Early Church*, IVP, 1982)

In view of this it is hardly surprising that the Stoical view won out. It seems that, by the third century AD, the only person who could be prosecuted for an abortion was the woman, and that not for harming the fetus (legally it was not yet a separate person) but because she had deprived her husband of progeny. For the husband to bear any guilt in the matter it was necessary to show first that he had consented to the abortion, and then that his wife had died as a result of it, or that he had used poisons—illegal in ancient Rome as heroin is today in the US.

This late Roman view of abortion stands in stark contrast to the Jewish position. Orthodox Judaism throughout the period covered by the Old and New Testaments had a profound respect for the sanctity of life. There was a deeply held conviction that a Jew's duty, far from destroying the weak or limiting the family, was to populate the earth—thus ensuring the survival of the race and the continuance of the divine presence on earth. This immediately distinguished them from the great civilizations of their age, for:

An exception to the frequent practice of abortion in antiquity was found among the Jews. Despite the absence of a specific condemnation or prohibition of abortion in their Scriptures, extensive research has discovered no mention of a non-therapeutic Jewish abortion in any texts of the Hebrew Bible or of any other Jewish literature through AD 500.

(Michael Gorman, *Abortion and the Early Church*, IVP, 1982)

Even so, at least two schools of thought developed within Judaism. Abortion might not be mentioned in the scriptures, but it had been covered in the collection of rabbinic teachings compiled around 200 AD as the Mishnah. Here a discussion of accidental (necessary) and deliberate feticide was carried on in the context of the legal and religious status of the fetus, understood by the two schools as dependent on the time of its *ensoulment*. This offered much the same distinction as that put forward by the Romans. However, for the Jews, whether a fetus was ensouled at birth, formation or conception could only be settled by the correct interpretation of scripture—and in particular of the first two chapters of Genesis.

It was the Palestinian school that leaned furthest to the pagan view by declaring that, since the fetus could not be regarded as a person, punishment for abortion should be decided on the basis of harm done to the mother. The Alexandrian school, affirming the personhood of the unborn but remaining flexible on the precise time of ensoulment, recommended punishment for harm done to the fetus, but according to its stage of development.

Christians who attempt to develop an ethic of abortion face the same problem as the Jews—a lack of definitive teaching in the Bible. But even if the New Testament is no more explicit than the Old there are certain principles drawn from both on which an ethic can be built.

For a start, the command to respect the sanctity of life (within defined limits) is established in the sixth commandment and thereafter regarded as absolute: all

that happens in the New Testament is that Thou Shalt
Not Kill becomes Thou Shalt Not Even Get Angry
Without Good Cause. Second, while the Bible contains
no explicit teaching about ensoulment it is clear that
writers of the Old Testament—notably David and
Jeremiah—considered their lives as separate individuals
to have started long before the moment of birth. The
same may be inferred in the New Testament from the
passage describing Mary's visit to Elizabeth, mother of
John the Baptist, when 'the babe leaped in her womb'
(Luke 1:41).

We can add to this the argument from dependency.
Looked at in social terms, it is simply a fact that all
human beings are dependent on others. That dependency
is at its greatest during infancy and old age. Then even
the most basic needs have to be met by others and, if
there is no one to meet them, death will inevitably ensue.

To a certain extent the obligation to help the very
young and the very old—and, we might add, the very
sick or the very poor—is built into human nature. Yet
there are many circumstances in which this sense of obligation will come second to self-interest. And there are
even some cultures—like the Roman—in which the abandonment of the weak is a matter of principle.

Such neglect is the antithesis of Christianity. 'Thou
shalt love the Lord thy God . . . and thy neighbor as
thyself' has constantly stressed the Christian obligation
to those in a state of dependency. It has been the inspi-
ration for the founding of countless hospitals, orphan-
ages, aid agencies and special care facilities. It is at the
heart of the faith.

The individuality of pre-natal life, as affirmed by the
Bible as well as modern science, is therefore not a fact
isolated from all moral consequences. Birth is an experience in life, not its beginning; not a significant change
in the level of dependency, merely in its nature. The
conclusion has to be, therefore, that if life is valued as a
matter of human right and divine command, aborting a
child before birth is morally equivalent to aborting it

after. The difference is that we call one abortion, the other murder.

This conclusion is shared by early Christian writers—first in the *Didache*, a manual of order for the church which explicitly forbids infanticide and abortion, and then in the more theological *Epistle of Barnabas* where the same prohibition is introduced with the same crucial command: 'Thou shalt love thy neighbor more than thy own life.' As far as these writers in the early second century were concerned, the fetus was more than a small prehuman organism. It was fully man.

But from what time?

The question of ensoulment still hangs over us as it did over the Romans and the Jewish rabbis. In some ways it is more pressing since it determines not only the legality of abortion but the legitimacy of genetic experiments that could conceivably be of enormous value in the saving of human life and the prevention of suffering. From a scientific point of view, once you reach the very early stages of life the choice is pretty arbitrary, as the Warnock Committee Report in Britain more or less admitted.

Fourteen days may be an adequate definition if you rely on scientific criteria to tell you that a fetus is not just a cluster of cells but a unique organism; but from the religious standpoint there is good reason for placing the crucial moment of ensoulment at conception. This after all is the moment at which the entire sequence of life begins, even if 'readable' signs of individuality, humanity, life, consciousness—call it what you will—do not appear till a later stage.

But these are, in the last analysis, only signs. If you could prove by some means that individuality actually entered a fetus, say, eighteen days after conception, that would not justify the conclusion that at seventeen days the fetus was a group of cells like any other group of cells and therefore expendable. From the time it was a fertilized egg and nothing else that tiny speck was destined to live just as surely as a growing boy is destined to become a man. It is alive.

This is the official position of several denominations, including my own, the Episcopalian Church of the USA. And it must imply that abortion is wrong from the first day of conception simply because, at any stage of its development, the unborn child has the chosenness and the rights of an individual soul.

But of course there are counter-arguments, and these generally fall into two categories—the defective child and the endangered mother.

In the first case the pressure to submit to an abortion is enormous now that genetic disorders can be identified in the fetus itself. Often the justification is that abortion is in the best interests of the child. But theologically this is a very dubious assertion.

At least one leading physician with a concern to work out a viable Christian ethic in this area—the Surgeon-General of the United States, Dr. C. Everett Koop—has taken his stand against it. He cites Moses at the burning bush: 'Who has made man's mouth? Or who makes the dumb, or deaf, or the seeing or the blind? Have not I, the Lord?'. (Exod. 4:11) It is not only the strong and the healthy who have a right to live or who can, with the love and attention of others, lead a life that is happy and fulfilled.

As to the endangered mother, almost all Christian churches—with the notable exception of the Roman Catholic—hold that in an either-or situation it is the mother's and not the child's life that should be preserved. Thus abortion may be justified as a matter of life for life if there is good reason to think the continuation of a pregnancy will be fatal to the mother.

Ethically less clear cut but still frequently approved is abortion after rape or incest. At stake here is not the mother's life *per se* but its quality in the face of a catastrophic situation for which she was not responsible. Emotional trauma, rejection of the child and, in the case of incest, possible genetic deformity may not individually justify terminating the pregnancy, but taken together they are often thought to make a cumulative case for abortion.

How far this concession of mitigating circumstances should be taken is hard to say and, as illustrated by Ludvig van Beethoven, much may be lost by taking it too far. This is why a Christian can never take this decision lightly, and very often Christians who are concerned to seek and obey God's will are led to refuse abortion. Take an example known to me. An Egyptian couple found in February of 1948 that they were expecting another child. They already had six, the oldest of whom was twenty. Although they were comparatively well-off, the prospect of a seventh seemed too much to bear. After much prayer, and perhaps also under the influence of the Muslim majority among whom abortion was common, they consulted a doctor with a view to obtaining an abortion.

The day before the wife went into the hospital something strange happened. She had been unable to sleep. There was no clear reason for it—the operation was a simple one with very little risk attached—and yet she found herself deeply troubled. Late in the evening they received a visit from their church pastor.

'I have a message from the Lord,' he said.

They could only look at him.

'You are not to terminate this pregnancy.'

'What!' exclaimed the husband. All the consequences of calling off the operation now rushed through his mind—cancelling with the hospital, the difficulties of coping while his wife carried the child, the danger of another birth. . . . In the end it was she who said what they were both thinking: 'But it's impossible. We've already made the arrangements.'

The pastor shook his head. 'I know, I know,' he said gently, 'but God is involved in this pregnancy. I have been praying for you, and He spoke to me. He told me to reassure you, and say that you will have both the health and the strength to cope with another child.' But the couple only gazed at him in dismay, and so he added, 'If God is in this, then you must obey Him.'

At that the wife laid down her arguments and took a simple step of faith. 'I believe you,' she said. 'We will phone the hospital immediately'.

God honored their obedience. In the end the pregnancy went far easier than the others, and on September 25th, 1948 she gave birth to a boy.

Mr and Mrs Youssef decided on the name Michael.

VII: DISARMAMENT: The Bomb in Your Pocket

Someone said to me recently, 'If World War Three ever comes it'll be the shortest war in history.'

In all likelihood it will be the end of history too—at least history as we know it: anyone who survived a full nuclear exchange and its grim, lingering consequences would have more pressing things to do than write his memoirs. In less than an hour nearly all the things making up the familiar and complex web of western civilization would be gone. Hospitals, schools, roads, railways, planes, shops, factories, fresh water, power, heat, light, money—all vanished, leaving behind them a sort of quadraplegic society, primitivized, unable to help itself, drastically and irrevocably changed.

That such an cataclysm can hardly be imagined in the comfort of America is only one of the paradoxes confronting us in the nuclear debate. Nobody could possibly want it to happen, and yet day by day we live with the fear that it will. The same bombs we say we'd be better without are hailed by many politicians as the guardians of international peace.

Everyone agrees there are more than enough nuclear warheads in the world, but we are told the only way to avoid having to use them is to make still more! Under the conditions of this logic rational discussion soon disappears beneath the waves of claim and counter-claim, leaving morality high and dry. What is the church to make of it all?

Of course it could be argued that, since the Bible is

over two thousand years old, Christians who attempt to develop a biblical view on the nuclear issue are boxing the air. Abortion, divorce and homosexuality may have been around in the ancient world, but a catapult is a far cry from a thermonuclear bomb. One feature all ages do have in common, though, is warfare, and it is by developing an understanding of this in the Judaeo-Christian tradition that we must begin in assessing the most modern methods war employs.

Something every kid in Sunday school knows about the Old Testament is that it's full of bloodthirsty killings. You don't have to read very far before people get knifed, run through or hewn to bits, sometimes thousands at a time.

Of course these biblio-nasties (to coin a phrase) have long since ceased to offend the man in the pew who, for the most part, treats them as he would a Shakespearean sonnet—with reverent inattention. But should he ever pause to think about them he will realize not just that they are violent, but worse, that they seem to be perpetrated at God's command. He will in fact make the same observation that led some early heretics to separate the loving Father of the New Testament from what they saw as the divine warlord of the Old.

It is sometimes said by way of excuse that the revelation of God's nature through history has been gradual. In other words, because love, forgiveness and the sacredness of human life came in a later module the Israelites couldn't be blamed for ignoring them. There is some truth in this, but it did not prevent the practice of war in Israel from having its own inner logic and morality.

According to the Old Testament account the Israelites acted as God's executors in bringing judgment on idolatrous nations, in the same way as the hangman has carried out the judgment of society on the murderer. Since God has the right both to judge and to select his instruments of justice the Canaanite wars cannot in this sense be immoral. In addition, the account makes it clear that the Israelites were taking back what was already their own possession, what had been promised to them through Abraham.

Taken together these points reveal the Canaanite wars as qualitatively different from most of the wars fought in the twentieth century; they were in fact holy wars, carried out at God's command to achieve a purpose God himself had ordained. There is no hint of imperialism, no notion of world conquest—simply an obedience to God's command and a claiming of his promise. And from this promise there eventually arose a quite different vision of Israel's relationship to other nations, led by a Messiah who would bring peace by suffering and self-sacrificing love.

This does not mean that every violent act portrayed in the Old Testament is a blueprint for the correct conduct of war. Nor does it mean that some of the later wars engaged in by Israel's and Judah's kings were legitimate in the terms laid down for the possession of the Promised Land. But it does mean that warfare as it was allowed for the people of Israel, was kept within defined limits and had to do with the establishment of justice. Also—and this is a vital point—whatever God taught Israel about war was taught to a nation in the context of the relationship between nations.

Here is one of the most significant differences between the Old and New Testaments. Jesus had very little to say about international relations. Insofar as he mentioned them at all he simply made predictions and observations: 'There will be wars and rumors of wars' (Mark 13:7); 'He who lives by the sword shall also perish by the sword' (Luke 21:24).

The main thrust of his teaching concerned not the relationship of nations, but of individuals. The parable of the good Samaritan, for instance, makes no reference to the status of Samaritans as a group, even to say that they should be accorded toleration and fair play. Instead one Jew, left for dead by robbers, is assisted by one Samaritan, and the moral derived from it is that all men as individuals should help others in need.

Thus the incomplete morality of the Old Testament ('You shall love your neighbor and hate your enemy') is superseded by the imperative of love: 'But I say to you, love your enemies and pray for those who persecute you. . . .' (Matt. 5:43).

So it was that, with Christ's words ringing in their ears, the early disciples preached the gospel of peace. With such an uncompromising command to love the aggressor, who would dare to take up the sword—even in obedience to the state? Listen to Tertullian, writing c.200 AD:

> We started yesterday and already we have filled the world and everything that belongs to you—the cities, apartment houses, fortresses, towns, market places, the camps themselves, your tribes, town councils, the imperial palace, the Forum. The only thing we have left you are the temples. You can count your armies; there is a greater number of Christians in one province! What kind of war would we, who willingly submit to the sword, not be ready and eager for despite our inferior numbers if it were not for the fact that according to our doctrine it is more permissible to be killed than to kill. (*Apology*, 37:4)

Tertullian's successor in the African church, Cyprian, was equally adamant that ' . . . after the reception of the Eucharist the hand is not to be stained with the sword and bloodshed' (from *On the Goodness of Patience*). And perhaps the greatest apologist of his age, Origen (185–254), the pupil of Clement of Alexandria

> . . . took a strong exception to any Christian involvement in war, and more than any other writer of the period . . . candidly faced the problems created by this issue, and . . . spelled out some of the implications of the pacifist position.
> (Louis J. Swift, *The Early Fathers on War and Military Service*, Michael Glazier, Inc., 1983)

One of the implications of this was that Christians became unpopular with their secular rulers. The state might declare war on whom it wished, but Christians wouldn't compromise their beliefs by fighting for it; before 170 AD they wouldn't even join the army.

This, said the state, was very unfair. After all, Christians enjoyed all the privileges the state bestowed on its citizens, and so it was their responsibility to defend it in its hour of need. As for Origen's excuse that Christians contributed to the state by combatting spiritual forces in prayer and turning enemies into allies, who had ever heard such a lot of nonsense?

It may not have been nonsense; but when in the fourth century Constantine was converted and Christianity became the official religion of the empire, a few theological chickens came home to roost. Conscientious objection in a pagan state was one thing; maintaining a policy of non-violence when every last soldier in the army was nominally a Christian was quite another. What if prayer failed and Rome fell to the barbarians? Could that really be God's will?

Contrary to appearances this wasn't entirely a loss of nerve on the part of Christian teachers who ought to have known better than to compromise. It was the inevitable result of applying individual ethics to the state. Killing people was wrong, certainly; but then taking a decision as a statesman that would result in the death or ruination of your subjects (for whom before God you were responsible) was clearly wrong as well.

You could sacrifice your own life, but who were you to sacrifice the lives of others? Slowly it began to dawn on the Christian community that in the political realm absolute morality had to be exchanged for relative, for choosing the lesser of two evils. As the church grew in wealth and influence, so the temptation to exploit this moral leeway increased.

The attempt to develop a workable ethic of state defense was quite sincere. However, in a way characteristic of the medieval church, it drew as much on the classical models of Plato and Aristotle as it did on Scripture. The final result, perfected by Thomas Aquinas in the thirteenth century, was the Just War Theory.

No one denied that war was an evil. But, the theory said, insofar as it was forced on the Christian state as a means of defending its people, it could be undertaken provided that certain conditions were observed. Since Aquinas the list of conditions has varied slightly, but most modern proponents of the Just War would agree on an absolute minimum of seven:

(1) That the decision for war must be made by a legitimate authority, that is, a legally constituted government. A possible if difficult exception to this occurs in cases of revolutionary insurrection where people believe a government has lost its right to govern through persistent disregard for justice and human rights. In such cases the authority to undertake a war may transfer to extra-governmental movements.

(2) That the war must be fought for a just cause, that is, with right intention. Force may only be used for the protection of justice and not for purposes of vengeance or domination, or in a way that makes a just peace unattainable.

(3) That the war must be declared only as a last resort. The use of force is only justified if all non-violent means of defense against injustice have been exhausted.

(4) That there must be a reasonable chance of success. In other words there must be some assurance that the good of justice will be achieved and that the last state of the belligerents and other affected parties will not be worse than the first.

(5) That the good to be achieved by a war outweighs any evil that results from it. This principle, also called *proportionality*, implies conversely that the force employed must not do greater harm than the evil it resists.

(6) That the war is waged with just means, that is, in accordance with natural and international law.

(7) That a war is declared before it is fought. Force must not be used until the aggressor has been given every possible opportunity to change the course of events, nor must it be used without serious political debate and the final consensus of the citizens of the defending country.

The difficulty of ensuring, in the emotionalism and chaos of war, that these conditions are fulfilled—and go on being fulfilled for the duration of the fighting—is almost insurmountable. This partly explains why the crusaders subsumed ideas of justice under the revived quasi-biblical concept of holy war. This actually sacrificed almost every principle of correct Christian conduct on the altar of territorial advantage, albeit an advantage ordained (supposedly) by God.

In the present time, especially in countries where the common soldier is likely to be an educated man, the question of the morality of warfare has again come to the fore. Interest in the Just War Theory has been renewed.

Vietnam must stand out as the classic example of a conflict abandoned because the participants no longer thought it just. The Falklands War of 1982 also demonstrates how hard it is for a nation already swung by notions of honour and retribution to give justice an impartial definition. In the end, it seems, even in countries with a Christian heritage, the Just War concept is invoked only when someone stands to gain by its invocation.

Until the end of the Second World War warfare remained essentially the same. True the machine gun, tank and long-range bomber had radically altered the scale and scope of the theatre, but at field H.Q. it was still the same old game of moving armies about and capturing ground.

The arrival of the nuclear age changed all that forever.

Suddenly there was a means of wiping out not just the army of an aggressor but his entire country, simply—*simply* by pressing a button. This was virtually absolute power. It flouted the few remaining rules in warfare just as surely as if a boxer carried a gun with him into the ring.

It had two immediate consequences: *one*, it brought home to the leaders of the major world powers that for the first time in history a war could decide not just which of two contestants won, but whether life as we know it would even continue on the planet; and *two*, it shifted the moral debate away from war in general and on to one particular weapon.

Looked at in detail the question about the Bomb turns out to be not one question but many, few of them with conclusive answers. What almost everyone agrees on is that nuclear weapons should not be used in a First Strike—that is morally execrable. But there are further dilemmas. Is it practicable to use nuclear weapons on the battlefield and expect no escalation to full nuclear exchange? If exchange does begin, and you didn't start it, is there any point in retaliating just to fulfil the terms of natural justice? Is it morally defensible even to *possess* nuclear weapons in a world where, according to the UN, countries already spend $17 billion every two weeks on arms—enough to keep every human being on the planet in food, water, education, health and housing for an entire year?

There can be no doubt that in an ideal world the £10 billion Britain is about to spend on Trident would be spent on poverty relief and development. But the crucial foundation in this discussion is the one Christians have been laying for centuries—the fact that the world is not ideal, but fallen, steeped in sin. Here at least Christian theology and pragmatism go hand in hand.

At the same time no Christian can be content with leaving the world as he finds it; we strive to make an ideal world, and in the nuclear age an ideal world must surely be one without nuclear weapons. From this perspective many of the complex questions can be reduced to a lowest common denominator: What is the best, safest way to reach the ultimate goal of complete, world wide nuclear disarmament?

The purist, standing in the pacifist tradition of the early Church fathers, would urge that because the very possession of nuclear weapons is wrong, a country should disarm unilaterally. This argument is not without its merits—after all, a real reduction in the number of nuclear weapons in the world is an achievement in itself and might act as a stimulus to multilateral reductions.

The problem is that it's risky. And remember, we don't want the quickest way to disarm, only the safest. A lot of Americans would say that unilateral disarmament is the military equivalent of putting a bottle of Scotch in front of an alcoholic—an almost irresistible temptation. The Soviets might not do the inevitable, but given four decades of tension and any realistic assessment of human nature there is no reason for them to abstain.

At the opposite end of the spectrum, and what prevails now, is the armed stalemate called *deterrence*. Where unilateral disarmament believes the best of an opponent, deterrence believes the worst. It takes no chances, and prides itself on a clean bill of nuclear health since the Second World War.

Critics of deterrence urge that it is not a state of affairs we can live with indefinitely. Peace is maintained at the cost of international tension which in turn encourages the growth of nuclear stockpiles. The crazy result is that weaponry is soon assessed not by its destructive power but by its *unnecessary* power—how many times you can shoot the man after the first bullet has killed him. Furthermore there exists a real danger of the horizontal proliferation of nuclear technology, of its spread to smaller nations desiring an independent defense in the nuclear world. This brings us to the crucial criticism of deterrence, for it relies very heavily on a belief, if not in the trustworthiness of an opponent, then at least in his rationality. With the USSR this may be justified. But what about Libya, Iran, or terrorist groups who may get their hands on a nuclear missile?

So are there any more options in attaining our goal? I think there are two. The first is the much-maligned Strategic Defense Initiative. Whatever its implications as a policy, there is no doubt that an operational SDI would neutralize the nuclear threat fast and efficiently. In order to avoid it becoming an appendage to American military capability, however, it is essential that the commitments made by Reagan in the 1984 pre-election debate with Walter Mondale should be followed through: SDI has in the end to be shared with the Russians. It has to be international, impartial.

Of course it is one thing to make promises, however sincere, but quite another to expect the Soviets to believe them. And that is why any sort of technological answer to nuclear weaponry—if it is not to be absorbed into the arms race must be backed up with positive political moves in the direction of multilateral disarmament. This could be accomplished with relative ease if the USA was willing to give a statement of intention and then stick by its word. A schedule of low risk policies—for instance stricter export lisenses on arms—would soon pave the way for more serious proposals on the reduction of stockpiles and the banning of underground tests.

This is not pacifism. It is not unilateral disarmament. It is not cowardice. It is not a betrayal of the United States' responsibility to protect the free world, or of Christianity determined to resist the ideological threat of communism. It is serious work to achieve the aim of the non-nuclear world without disturbing the international balance or asking any one country to compromise its defense commitments.

Behind it, of course, is the distinctly Christian belief that people were not created as Americans and Russians, slaves and freemen, blacks and whites, but as men and women in the image of God. We perhaps get closest to seeing this when we imagine the Soviet citizen walking in the park on a Sunday afternoon, holding hands with his wife, playing with his children. Here is something deeper than ideology and yet ideology—be it the ideology of

freedom, of communism, or the Crusade—all too easily
obscures it.

Should we allow this sort of doublethink to take place
when we know that disarmament is first and foremost a
spiritual issue, raising fundamental questions about the
way we see our fellow men? That is why the church must
examine its conscience, know the issues, make use of its
influence and, most of all, pray that in a game of imposs-
ibly high stakes policies are formulated not on the basis
of fear or greed, but on Christian truth.

The church must also hope. That's not a word you hear
very often among anti-nuclear campaigners. Yet it is a
fundamental Christian belief that whether Rome is falling
to the barbarians or the missiles are on their way God is
still in control of the universe.

Human freedom is contained within the bounds of
God's sovereign will. Satan cannot exploit the arms crisis
to ruin creation; he could do nothing to Job without
God's permission, and when he offered Christ the world
in exchange for his worship Christ answered emphatically
that the world wasn't Satan's to give away. Nothing will
happen to God's creation that is not part of his purpose
to allow, and that covers the threat of nuclear holocaust
as much as anything else.

At the same time, this hope is not just for the present
world. The disciples who were so excited about the
miracles they performed were tersely reminded of their
real priorities: 'Nevertheless do not rejoice in this . . . .
but that your names are written in heaven' (Luke 10:20).
No earthly joy is worth the joy to come, no justice worth
the justice of heaven, no death more fearsome than being
cast into Hades.

That is why the Church must always seek first the
Kingdom of God. Evangelism is the key to bringing that
world's end which, unlike the nuclear holocaust, is a
positive fulfilment of history. 'When the gospel of the
Kingdom is preached to all nations as a testimony to all
the world, *then the end will come*' (Matt. 24:14).

VIII: CHURCH AND STATE: The Great Divide

It's sometimes said that talking about politics and religion is the best way of falling out with your friends. True or not (I leave it up to you to find out) what the average American believes about God and the government are likely to count among his most deeply held convictions.

He is also likely to have strong views on the relationship between the two; he may go out of his way (as many do) to say that moral opinions based on religious beliefs have no right to dictate state policy on matters such as abortion and censorship. To deny that these are issues for the individual conscience, he will say, is to deny a fundamental freedom—and to show contempt for the founding fathers whose intent in the First Amendment was clearly that church and state should be separated.

Whether he is right is another question. However delicate the founding fathers construed the marriage of church and state to be, they were certainly not pressing for divorce, nor did any take place. A constitution bound to strict religious neutrality would not have proclaimed its trust in the almighty on its coinage or allowed its citizens to pledge an oath of Allegiance as 'one nation, under God'.

Not only that, federal government employs chaplains in the armed forces, the Senate and the House of Representatives both have chaplains and both open their sessions with prayer. That is not a state divorced from religion—unless the divorcees still share the same house. It proves the marriage is still in good shape.

CHURCH AND STATE 73

At the same time it is a marriage with tensions and arguments.

Everett Sileven, a pastor from Nebraska, has recently spent time in jail for not registering the teachers at his church-run elementary school—on the grounds that registration, by restricting the free exercise of religion, would be unconstitutional. In Michigan Judge Randall Heckman has risked removal from office by refusing abortion to a pregnant thirteen-year-old girl. At every level, from local to federal government, from the single conscience to the entire denomination, church and state suspect one another of trespassing on their respective domains, and countless times have arrived at confrontation.

But long before Christianity and government came into any formal liaison, even before Nero took up his fiddle and his matches, Christians were wondering what to do with the state. They were trying to work out if it was basically a good or bad thing, and how to respond to the demands it made of them. In the canon of scripture three very distinct and important perspectives were arrived at.

The first (not so much arrived at as given) came from Christ himself in response to the touchy issue of taxes paid to an occupying power: 'Render to Caesar the things that are Caesar's, and to God the things that are God's' (Mark 12:17). The church was never meant to be a theocracy. Duties toward God are not to be neglected, but in the life of the Christian disciple Caesar too has his privileges which include, at the very least, the right to levy a tax.

The assumption seems to be that in his relation to the state the Christian functions like any just citizen. He does not need to make civil rule part of his responsibility because that is already, by God's arrangement, taken care of by somebody else. Christianity is not to advance by altering the structure of the state but by transforming the individuals who compose it: a little leaven leavens the whole lump.

The implications of this are spelled out by Paul in Romans 13:

> Let every person be subject to the governing authori-
> ties. For there is no authority except from God, and
> those that exist have been instituted by God. Therefore
> he who resists the authorities resists what God has
> appointed, and those who resist will incur
> judgment. . . . Would you have no fear of him who is
> in authority? Then do what is good and you will receive
> his approval, for he is God's servant for your good.
> But if you do wrong, be afraid, for he does not bear
> the sword in vain; he is the servant of God to execute
> his wrath on the wrongdoer. Therefore one must be
> subject, not only to avoid God's wrath but also for the
> sake of conscience. For the same reason you pay taxes,
> for the authorities are ministers of God, attending to
> this very thing. Pay all of them their dues, taxes to
> whom taxes are due, revenue to whom revenue is due,
> respect to whom respect is due, honor to whom honor
> is due. (Romans 13:1–7)

In Paul's reckoning secular authorities are to be obeyed
for the simple reason that God has put them there; they
are God's servants 'for your good' and 'to execute wrath'.

Thus is created the awful paradox of church-state
relations, for the word *diakonos* (minister, servant) is
used in the New Testament both of the secular authorities
and of the Christian church. Both act on behalf of God,
though one belongs to the Kingdom of Heaven and the
other (certainly in Paul's time) to the kingdom of the
world. Yet, Paul says, in day to day life the heavenly
Kingdom must be *subject* to the worldly!

The most straightforward interpretation of this—the
positivist position—is that Christian obedience to the
decrees of state must be absolute and unquestioning, with
the consequence that the state becomes a source of ethical
guidance as well as legal authority. So long as it enforces
laws that are just and fair a Christian can live with this
quite happily. But as soon as the state acts in contravention of divine law—say by adopting a policy of anti-
semitism—he will find himself in the awkward position of

having to obey (because the state as God's servant tells him to) laws that he knows from Christian teaching are evil and unjust.

He may comply through fear, but fear alone will make him do it. Intellectually he can reach only two conclusions: either God has gone back on all that He said about himself in the Bible, or the state is misusing the authority He entrusted to it. This second conclusion is the one that led Karl Barth to denounce Hitler in the famous Barmen Declaration of 1934 and Dietrich Bonhoeffer to take part in the resistance movement.

The common belief behind both actions was that there may come a point when a government proves itself unfit to rule, when it is no longer a legitimate state and is therefore not deserving of the Christian obedience bestowed on it by Paul in Romans 13. Far from equating ethical guidance with the decisions of the state this **legitimist** position holds that a state must itself be subject to the moral law. Only when it obediently upholds that law should Christians obey it; the disobedient state must be disobeyed. The Philippines is a good example of this.

The distinction between a good and a bad government may be simple to apply under dictatorship, but rule in a democracy is not so easily assessed. At what point could most Christians agree that Reagan's or Thatcher's government had forfeited its right to govern? Is it not true that reasonably good governments sometimes pass bad laws, and that many democratic decisions that look bad from one point of view can be morally justified from another?

Accepting that ethical issues in government are complex and muddy brings us to a third, **responsive** interpretation of Romans 13, recommending not the wholesale acceptance or rejection of the *state* but an ethical judgment of its particular actions. The latitude for this interpretation is found in the word Paul uses for 'submit'. It is not one of the more absolute terms available in Greek—*peitho or hupakouo*—but a word of military origin referring to order and rank.

Accepting our place in society means recognizing the

sovereignty of the civil authorities, but does not commit us to indiscriminate obedience. We obey God first and the state second, and we apply this ordering of our priorities to each situation as it arises.

> And when they had brought them they set them before the council. And the high priest questioned them, saying, 'We strictly charged you not to teach in this name, yet here you have filled Jerusalem with your teachings and you intend to bring this man's blood upon us.' But Peter and the apostles answered, 'We must obey God rather than men. . . .' (Acts 5:27–29)

But all that the Bible has to say about church and state was said long before their marriage or even their courtship began. That fateful union, suggested by Constantine, sealed by Theodosius and maintained on and off in western culture ever since, has raised a further set of questions to which the New Testament writers did not address themselves. These concern the proper definition of roles for church and state in a society that has somewhat a Christian heritage.

The great temptation as soon as the word 'Christian' is applied to the state is to assume that the separation implicit in Christ's teaching and in Romans 13 may be waived. So the secular state is God's servant? Then how much better it must be when that state is converted and its servanthood subsumed under that of the saints! 'Do you not know,' says Paul, 'that we are to judge angels? How much more, matters pertaining to this life?' (I Cor. 6:3).

Of course the big catch is that when it comes to the business of good government the saints may not be a howling success. The context of Paul's question is precisely that the Corinthians were *unable* to judge the matters of this life. 'I say this to your shame. Can it be that there is no man among you wise enough to decide between members of the brotherhood, but brother goes

to law against brother, and that before unbelievers?'
(I Cor. 6:5,6).

Notwithstanding, some Christians have promoted the
idea of church-as-state very eagerly, among them many
of the early colonists in America. But legislating faith,
giving God Caesar's portion as well as His own, quickly
ran into trouble when apostasy set in. The state of
Connecticut found itself fining those who failed to attend
church on Sunday and New Hampshire's first constitution
saddled entire towns with the responsibility to elect
congregational ministers.

This was bad news for both the church and the state:
the Kingdom of God cannot, by definition, be furthered
by legislation—that is simply a reversion from faith to the
Law. The kingdom of the world, which will always include
unbelievers, cannot be expected to abide long by a legal
code based on religious premises it does not share. What
results is a tyranny of religion damaging to religious and
irreligious citizens alike.

But if church-as-state is an unworkable ideal, the
opposite extreme to which it all too frequently gives
way—the state-as-church—is a familiar political reality.
In its worst form this is the adoption of both roles by a
state in which all adherence to theistic belief has been
officially abandoned. Thus the Christian church is
suppressed or taken over while the state promulgates its
own ideological substitute for religion: Caesar becomes
God.

But the state can take over the church in far more
subtle ways than that. In Europe during the sixteenth and
seventeenth centuries, when Christian faith was more or
less ubiquitous, distinctions between brands of Christianity were more significant than that between the sacred
and the secular. In fact, the form of religious belief upheld
by a country or community often served as shorthand for
its political identity—a phenomenon that survives today
in a weakened form in the conflict between Protestants
and Catholics in Northern Ireland.

Thus, for instance, when the Church of England was

established by Henry VIII in 1534 it became a bolster against the political challenge first of the English Catholics and then of the Puritans. Theological arguments were passionately contended, but in the end it was not theology that mattered. The Church of England was the religious expression of a community under siege; in the lean years it stood as a symbol of unity, in the good years it became an instrument of oppression.

This concurrence of religious belief and political power, characteristic alike of medieval Catholicism, Luther's Germany and the English Reformation, caused weaker minority groups to rally round the flags of dissent as a matter of conscience and political necessity. This was the heritage of the first settlers in America; and since they sought a place in the New World where their faith—untainted by the long embrace of the state—might be practised in liberty, it is no surprise that in 1787 the founding fathers made liberty the keynote of the Constitution.

They effectively separated the *functions* of church and state in such a way that the old evils would never rise again. Not only was there to be no *official* religion (in spite of the fact that nearly all those who framed the Constitution were Christians), but *the state could place no restrictions on the religious beliefs of its citizens*. Church and state were thus protected from one another: the church could not rule through the state, nor could the state force any man, Christian or otherwise, to betray his conscience.

The government was free to rule, the church was free to worship and evangelize, and everything was rosy in the constitutional garden. At first sight it seems as though our average American is absolutely justified in his view that Christian morality shouldn't be allowed to interfere in politics.

Or is he?

We have already seen how there are doors in the wall of separation between church and state. The Church influences the state insofar as prayer is an official feature on the agenda of Senate and the House of Representatives. And most of us would agree that in a case like the Jonestown massacre, where a religious group is disobeying the law, the state should interfere with the church.

But the relationship goes deeper than that.

While the roles of state and church have been carefully divided, state and *religion* remain inseparable. The values underlying the American Constitution are transparently religious. There is no doubt from the writing of its authors that they themselves were at the very least deists who regarded religion as central to the concepts of justice and freedom—and to the education of citizens whose character would make a pluralistic democracy work.

Of course a great many people with no religious beliefs would agree that a government should promote justice and freedom for the good of its people—but it is only religion, and specifically Christian theism, that provides a coherent basis for this view.

A greater power to whom government is responsible and not a quasi-impartial secular humanism, is the foundation on which the American constitution is built. We are not just one nation, but one nation *under God*.

Here is the specific and political rationale (as opposed to the general and theological rationale) for Christian participation in the democratic process. If we live under a constitution committed to the aims of what from a biblical standpoint is good government, we have a responsibility to see that those aims are promoted, not as a matter of sectarian interest but for the good of the nation. This motivation of course is frequently called in question by the liberal humanists—hence the advertisement run in the *Washington Post* by Planned Parenthood with the caption 'Abortion is something personal, not political'. Strictly speaking, abortion is neither a personal nor a political issue, but a moral one. However, that being granted, the fight against abortion on demand must—by anyone who cares about the moral foundation of the state—be carried into the political arena. No one would deny this argument if we were talking about child-molesting or infanticide. The only reason such a fuss is made about abortion (to give one example of this sort of issue) is that popular opinion has ceased to regard it as a moral evil.

This is a serious problem.

Does duty bid us to legislate what the majority want, or what from the biblical point of view is ethically correct? A democratic system seems to demand the former. As Mario Cuomo, governor of New York, said in his speech at Notre Dame in 1984, the man who passes a law at odds with public consensus is asking to have his law scoffed at.

But does this absolve us, as Christians or as citizens, of the responsibility to urge on society what is morally right? Of course not—we would betray our commitment both to the Bible and the Constitution if we did not do so. The question is: How are we best to go about it?

Incidentally, we come here to one of the major differences between the British and American approaches to church-state relations. Britain's is very clearly a post-Christian society: church membership has been falling since the turn of the century and in 1979 stood at just over 6.5 million (out of a total population of 54 million) with only half that number in actual attendance. Partly through this widespread abandonment of the church, and partly through the weakening of the connection between political identity and religion among minority congregations, the Church of England has become far more mild-mannered and tolerant.

In fact, far from being the official religion of government or even, as it has often been dubbed, the Tory Party at prayer, the Anglican Church has gained a reputation for siding with the poor and carping about high unemployment. This tendency has caused government ministers to discount church reports like the recent *Faith in the City* (1985) as predictable, left wing and misinformed. The attitude government takes to Christian comment of this sort is well summed up by a Conservative MP quoted in the *Church Times*, January 17, 1986, in the context of the

Shops Bill, a contentious measure designed to liberalize Sunday trading. He noted: 'We already have enough trouble with bishops without turning parish pulpits into campaigning centres against this legislation.'

But for all the discomfiture caused to the government by socially conscious clergymen, Christianity in Britain is hardly a major political force. Pressure groups like Christian CND and Festival of Light may be noisy but they lack the broad base of support necessary for real clout.

Not so Christianity in America. Out of ten people in the United States, nine will tell you they believe in God, eight will say they are Christians. And that amounts to a slumbering giant in the electorate whose conscience can potentially be stirred by moral issues—political dynamite, as the politicians are very well aware.

But the problem with dynamite is that it can blow up in your face. It is one thing to recognize a latent desire (in a population) to live by the highest principles of justice, but it is quite another to see that desire realized in legislation. For one thing there are any number of Big Bad Wolves in the world of politics who are willing to wear Granny's spectacles and put her knitting in their laps for the sake of eating up Little Red Riding Hood.

This leads to the inevitable problem of seeing the motive behind the rhetoric. But also—and worse—there is a tendency to cast policies in the language of religion to woo the Christian vote. The moral content of a proposed policy may on close scrutiny prove to be very dubious, but the fact is few people have the time, resources or intellectual apparatus to discern this.

And so, what they go by isn't the product but the package. And packaging—especially if it 'looks like' patriotism or national security, issues close to the American heart—can be very attractive indeed. The result is that a pot pourri of political ideas, some religious, some secular, is brought inside the church and sanctified as Christian. It is American culture dressing in the robes of religion.

It is important to realize here that we are not necessarily talking about sincere, innocent Christians being manipulated by nasty, scheming, atheistic serpents. The entire process can happen within the church. Policies advocated by the Moral Majority, for instance, may pose as straightforward biblical options. The fact is they arise in churches which already have a very clear political orientation, and arrive on the Christian voter's doorstep in an intellectually sealed package.

The unspoken implication is that the policies presented are for all intents and purposes the 'right' ones. And if the Christian is tempted to think them a touch too strident, a touch too close to the potent creeds of capitalism and nationalism, he can put his mind at rest with the thought that they are, by the sure word of his Christian brothers, *biblical*.

In the political arena in general the arrival of aggressive fundamentalist Christianity, pressing for the recovery of moral absolutes, challenging the legal accommodation of deviant lifestyles, backing pro-life candidates, has ironically produced fear. Many fear that movements like Moral Majority seek to turn America from a pluralistic democracy into a Christian state—precisely what the (Christian) founding fathers strove to make impossible.

The backlash was inevitable and drew on the same instinctive feelings that wrote the First Amendment into the constitution. The church, it seemed, could not take part in state affairs without wanting to take over. So, like the child who cannot join another's game without spoiling it, it must be separated.

This calls for a serious re-evaluation of the methods employed by American Christians in leading their culture. Nearly every issue treated in this book is of concern to state and church alike. In a country whose very constitution is founded on the principles of Christian theism, and where the majority of citizens class themselves as believers, correct participation in the political process is a matter of paramount importance.

The church leads by example, by evangelism, by personal ministry; but it must also lead—corporately as

well as individually—by working for the common good
through the democratic system. Two things are needed
for this to be done effectively.

One, we need an honest assessment of our own attitudes in the light of biblical teaching. We can't start
poking around for splinters in anyone else's eye before
we've got the log out of our own. Nor can we expect any
spiritual power behind our ministry to the world if our
house is divided and our principles compromised. Salt
without saltness will soon let the fish go stale—a nasty
business for everybody.

The *second* thing we need is grace. The simple fact is,
Christians aren't as clean and clever as they sometimes
like to think. A paradise created by a people of God still
imperfect would eventually turn into hell on earth. This
is undoubtedly one reason why the founding fathers gave
every American the right to contract out of other Men's
dreams.

True, it is the calling of the church to lead its culture.
But we acknowledge too that we are one-eyed men in
the kingdom of the blind, and liable every now and again
to fall into the pit with the rest. Called to lead we are
ourselves led, and therefore imperfect; but when the
perfect comes, the imperfect will pass away and what we
now see in a mirror dimly will be seen face to face.

Let's pray that we will be more ready for that 'revol-
ution' than we were for Galileo's.